CHURCHILL'S
SECRET AGENT

CHURCHILL'S SECRET AGENT

Josephine Butler
Codename 'Jay Bee'

Blaketon-Hall

First published in Great Britain 1983 by
Blaketon-Hall Limited,
11 North Street, Ashburton, Devon

ISBN 0-907854-02-8

Reproduced, printed and bound in Great Britain by
Hazell Watson & Viney Ltd, Aylesbury, Bucks

Contents

Acknowledgements

My thanks go to Esther Latham for her help in making this book readable. I am inclined to be factual, but she has made it human.

I owe much to Gwen Wilkinson and Betty Bailey, who encouraged me to make this record of my experiences in the Secret Circle; also to Peggy Bennett, who typed the manuscript. These Durham friends are magnificent.

This book is dedicated to the men and women who served in Resistance against the Nazi evil who are unknown and will remain unknown, and to the memory of the man who inspired and believed in them, the late Sir Winston Spencer Churchill.

1

How It All Began

An hour before midnight in the Autumn of 1943 I was crouching among some ornamental bushes in the grounds of a large house just outside Limoges in the supposed Occupied Zone of France, waiting for the right moment to begin the action which was to complete my latest assignment.

Since the Spring of 1942 I had been a member of Winston Churchill's Secret Circle, crossing backwards and forwards between France and England on various missions, but this was the first time that I had been asked to try to bring someone out of France. The man in question was a member of an important French family who was reputed to be a Nazi sympathiser and working with the Germans. With the help of my special Lyon group of Resistance workers I was to attempt to get him out of France by means of an escape route.

It was very peaceful here in the gardens. The air was becoming cool but it was a fine night and the clear sky was bright with stars. As I warily watched the house from my hiding place my thoughts were very mixed. Here was I, a trained and qualified doctor of medicine and a great respecter of law and order, sitting on the ground on a private estate in France with the firm intention of kidnapping the owner. It was contrary to all my principles, but it was an order, and I would carry it out if possible. The gruelling realities of my last assignment were still very vivid in my mind. I had just come through a testing experience, and the fact that I had succeeded gave me added confidence. I had met with physical pain and danger, and had overcome them.

We had arranged to put our plan into action just after midnight, and as I waited in silence I began to think back over the events in my life which had linked together over the years and prepared me for the task of serving my country in this way.

It really all began when I was eight years old. My parents decided that I was growing unruly and sent me to a convent school in Bruges. French became my first language.

My childhood was a very happy one. We lived in Buckingham-shire for a time, where I was born, then later we moved to Wiltshire. I grew up with six brothers, with the result that I was somewhat of a tomboy. Four of my brothers were killed in active service but as children we were very close to each other. Under the influence of my father, a truly fine man, we were brought up to respect Duty, Law and Justice. We had a German governess whom we all disliked intensely. She was a relic of the Victorian era and a strict disciplinarian, verging on being a tyrant, but my mother thought that this type of training was good for us. After being with us for two years, however, Fräulein departed in disgust, describing us as 'hooligan children'.

One day we had been squabbling over our toys and my father talked to us seriously about 'sharing', and how it was wrong and not in keeping with true love and compassion to worship our possessions. My brothers and I decided among ourselves that Fräulein was guilty of worshipping her hair. We had noticed that every day after the midday meal she loosened her plaits, which she wore braided round her head, and stroked them lovingly as she rested. We were always made to lie flat on our backs on the floor during this time 'for the good of our spines', and she usually fell asleep. We agreed that Fräulein must be taught not to be 'possessive' about her hair, and laid our plans accordingly.

The plaits must be cut off, and my second-eldest brother decreed that I should help him to do the wicked deed. We borrowed some small garden shears from the gardener's tools without his knowledge, as we knew that scissors would not be strong enough to sever the thick plaits quickly, and speed was essential. The next time that the unsuspecting Fräulein was enjoying her after-dinner nap we crept up and chopped off the offending plaits.

My father punished us severely by confiscating our most treasured possessions, but when poor Fräulein departed in fury I don't think any of us was sorry to see her go.

Fräulein was superseded by Mademoiselle, a delightful vivacious girl called Colette who came from the North of France. She had red hair and beautiful green eyes. She was deeply religious, but although she was a Roman Catholic and we were Protestant she did not attempt to influence us. One day when I was eight I was out walking with Colette and saw a carter ill-treating his horse. I have always loved animals, and I quite literally saw red. I leapt upon the man, dragged him to the ground, and hammered his head on the road. It was after this incident that I was sent to the convent in Bruges.

From this time on I began to perfect my French and to develop the retentive memory and photographic mind which proved so invaluable during my years of service with the Secret Circle. As I was the only Protestant receiving tuition at the convent at that time, it was arranged that I should not take prayers with the rest of the pupils. The nuns and the Mother Superior, who were gentle, educated women, arranged my separate prayer time. I was often left on my own to read passages from the New Testament and to learn hymns, and I discovered that I could memorise a whole page, so that when questioned about what I had been reading I could quote long passages word for word. I could actually see words that I had read long after the book was closed. Of course there are disadvantages to this gift, as I can also remember and visualize all the horrors I have seen.

During the First World War our convent personnel and pupils were transferred from Belgium to the South of France, to Menton. My father had an estate between Nice and Grasse, so that I was now near home. The war seemed a long way away, but there were many uniformed men in the district. Quite a number of British villa-owners had given their homes to be used for the benefit of wounded officers of the Allies, where they could convalesce.

When I was eighteen we were joined by a cousin whom we had not seen before. Florence was two years younger than myself, and our mothers had been twin sisters. We were told that as her parents were both dead, she would be coming to live with us from then on. I well remember our first meeting.

I was looking at a girl of my own height - rather above average - with straight, very dark brown hair, a large, mobile mouth and rather big teeth. A pair of wide open hazel eyes gazed into mine with an expression of astonishment that must have been reflected in my own. I was looking at my double.

If we could have known at that moment the strange way that our resemblance was to affect our future lives, we would have been even more astonished.

There were of course a few superficial differences. My cousin had a fringe which I admired and decided to imitate - actually I went one better and had my hair cut in a peaked or 'Mephistopheles' fringe. She wore her hair tied at the back with a big bow, while mine was plaited and coiled round my head. My dark eyebrows were thick; she had plucked hers to be in the latest fashion. She had my long shapely legs - I was rather vain about my legs - but I noticed with a flash of unworthy pleasure that her stockings were not as elegant as mine.

Our identical appearance was a source of amusement to my brothers. They said that, as doubles, we ought to have the same name. Mine was Josephine, so they nicknamed her Jo, and the name stuck. (The nickname they had always used for me was 'Padre's Delight', as they said I was a 'sucker for sob stories'.) My brothers adored Jo. She always attracted men; women seemed to be envious of her. Mentally we were not at all alike. I had become rather serious-minded, while Jo was very light-hearted and gay. She loved dancing and was an excellent mimic.

Jo went to Switzerland to finish her education. Her ambition was to take up child welfare work and nursing and in this she qualified, but did not continue the work. She married quite young, was widowed after three years, married again, and once more became a widow. Both husbands were killed in car accidents.

After the First World War I decided that I would like to read Medicine and Sociology at the Sorbonne. I had heard from various sources that this sociology course embraced a great deal of practical work besides the lectures, and I wanted to learn about people - their minds as well as their bodies. I was accepted for the Sorbonne and eventually qualified as a Doctor of Medicine with a degree in Sociology. I enjoyed my years of study, and found that I did learn a great deal about people - their vices and their virtues. I also took part in many sporting and athletic activities during this time and became an expert in ju-jitsu. I learnt fencing, but did not have the calculating mind to excel in this kind of sport. I was a good high jumper and tennis player, and above all I could walk for miles without effort.

After leaving the Sorbonne I joined a Cancer Research Unit as I had decided to take up research instead of general practice or a hospital appointment. I joined a private clinic in which Thierry de Martel was the leading surgeon; it was a building in the Rue des Invalides. Thierry was a brilliant surgeon and had a great reputation as an obstetric surgeon, but he was also very interested in brain surgery, cancer and diseases of the blood. He often said that most diseases could be traced by a study of the blood of patients.

Cancer is the most malignant of diseases and I became

enthralled with the work of research. We studied many of the patients from the Marie Curie Hospital who were suffering from terminal cancers. I visited Germany frequently during the late Twenties. There were some very great surgeons there, many of whom were Jews. It was becoming noticeable that Hitler intended to get rid of the Jewish people in Germany and that the poison of anti-Semitism was spreading rapidly throughout the country. I heard Germans whom I had thought good and intelligent people saying such things as: 'Jews and Slavs are sub-humans and must be dealt with by the Super Race of Germans.'

When I visited Germany in the early Thirties there were uniforms in evidence everywhere. Even von Ribbentrop and his colleagues at the Foreign Office were strutting about in Nazi uniform. Himmler's S.S. was growing fast. His intention was to build up a Nordic Empire with pure Germans whose ancestry was traced back to the seventeenth century to recruit those who had no trace of foreign blood in their veins. The Waffen S.S., formed later, was augmented with foreigners who believed in the Nazi creed but were Germans of partly foreign descent.

Hitler's conception of Nationalism had a very strong appeal to a nation who had not forgotten their defeat in 1918 and the humiliating terms of the Peace Settlement, nor the terrible period of inflation which had ruined so many of them. The industrialists supported Hitler because of their fear of Communism, and the Army officers because they shared his dream of restoring Germany's military power. The rearmament programme gave a much-needed boost to employment. In 1933 the Jews were turned out of the professions and their places filled by so-called Aryans.

But in 1934 one man alone spoke out against Nazi aggression: Winston Churchill. He was labelled a warmonger.

Europe was changing. I could feel the evil building up. Even in Paris we saw many German V.I.P.s and many French politicians mixing with them; and we wondered ... I listened to the gossip of Paris. It was rumoured that Hitler had a wonderful astrologer who advised him, and that he had a list of countries and the dates on which they would be invaded, starting with Austria and ending with Britain in the Autumn of 1941. In 1938, during the Munich crisis, I decided to return to Britain. It meant giving up for a time the work I loved, but I loved my country more and I was very sure we would soon be at war with Germany.

Thierry de Martel, the director of the clinic in Paris, said that if war came he would move the clinic to the South of France.

However, events moved too quickly. There were people in Paris who were working with the Germans. Many great families were afraid of Communism and had adopted the National Socialism of Germany. When France capitulated in June 1940 it was too late for Thierry de Martel to get out. He destroyed our equipment and burned all our notes so that they could not be misused by the Germans. Then, like many others, he committed suicide rather than give them a 'blank cheque'. These people would have been used by the Nazis, and they preferred to die.

2

The Secret Place

When I returned to England in 1938, I felt that in the event of war the newly re-formed force of F.A.N.Y. (First Aid Nursing Yeomanry) would enable me to give my best service. I was considered a good driver, and my knowledge of medicine would help.

After the Munich crisis the London County Council began to recruit men and women for part-time Civil Defence. They had their own Ambulance Service and Fire Service and it was easy to recruit auxiliaries without a great deal of publicity. They were all taught First Aid. Undoubtedly it was thought that if Germany became an enemy she would attack London, especially the East End of London where there were many Jewish people. In the training of this particular Civil Defence the large number of Jewish taxi-drivers who joined was noticeable.

My cousin Jo, who had been in England since 1931, had married again after the loss of her first husband. I had married the cousin of her second husband in 1932, so we now had the same surname. Jo joined the Civil Defence because she wanted to be on the Home Front, and she did splendid work during the heavy raids on London.

When war was declared each county in England had its own Civil Defence. London was almost ready, as the L.C.C. had already a trained force of firemen, police and ambulance personnel. Many of these became full-time Civil Defence, others remained part-time until later, when conscription was introduced and they had to serve full-time or join other services. There were many part-time people attached who were in reserved occupations which excluded them from call up but who gave up their leisure time to serve their country. During the raids on London - and the first was, as expected, on the East End of London - the Civil Defence proved itself. Firemen, policemen, ambulance drivers and demolition workers; both men and women were heroic.

After the capitulation of France F.A.N.Y. was disbanded as a voluntary force and became a paid one. Many women left and joined other services. One group started the M.T.C. (Mechanised Transport Corps) a unit which drove V.I.P.s and helped to evacuate hospitals during air raids. They certainly were the real endurance drivers; driving with only half side-lights and an absence of road signs and names was a nightmare which they quickly overcame. As a member of F.A.N.Y. I drove many V.I.P.s, among them Sir Stafford Cripps. He was a member of the War Cabinet and he liked a silent driver.

After the air raids on London had lessened I thought I would like to get back to medicine. I felt I would be of more use here than driving V.I.P.s. I could not do this, however, as I was told to report to the Ministry of Economic Warfare (M.E.W.) in Berkeley Square. This Ministry was a hive of industry, housed in a block of luxury flats and consequently very comfortable. I had to see a 'Doctor H' who told me that I would be dealing with maps of Europe. I explained that I knew very little about maps except those used for driving, but he said that I would soon learn. I was a civilian again, and at first found the work rather dull. As time went on, however, the work became much more interesting and I was told that it was very important to S.O.E. (Special Operations Executive). This was the first time I had heard of this organisation. I did not ask questions. All my life I have found that if you do not pry you get the information in time.

I worked alone and found that the various departments had taken over individual large flats on many floors of the Ministry. I liked being on my own. I had a very large room in which I worked and was visited from time to time by men working in other rooms. These men were expert map-makers and map-readers from the British Museum and they advised and helped me very much. I realised that the men and women in the various departments were obviously experts in their own field, and I could not help wondering why *I* had been chosen.

One day shortly after I had started work in this section a man was shown into my room and I was asked if I would allow him to wait there for a time as there was no other room available. I agreed, offered him a chair, and went back to my desk. He was immaculately dressed, very good-looking and about forty-five years of age. He also had a military bearing, which I recognised at once as five of my brothers were in the Services.

After a short silence, during which I got on with my writing, he asked suddenly, 'Are you a civil servant?'

'Heaven forbid!' I said feelingly.

'Don't you like civil servants?'

'I haven't really given it much thought,' I said, 'but I've always felt they were very efficient, machine-like people, and I don't want to be a machine.'

He was silent for a while, then asked me what I did, what exactly was my work. I felt that he was prying, and was rather annoyed.

'I do this and that,' I said.

He smiled, but persisted. 'And what does this and that consist of?'

'Just what I said. This and that.'

It must have been clear that what I meant was, 'Mind your own business', but even that didn't silence him. 'But you must have a status,' he insisted.

'Oh yes,' I said, 'I have a status. I am a Dogsbody.'

He smiled disarmingly. 'I suppose I deserved that.'

'You should know better than to ask questions,' I said firmly. 'Now if you'll excuse me I must get on with my this and that.'

I felt that he was watching me and was about to ask if he would like something to read when he stood up and went to the door saying, 'I think they'll be ready now. Goodbye. It has been a pleasure to meet you.' I merely nodded and went on with my work. I did wonder, however, what such an obviously military type was doing out of uniform.

A few days after this incident I was taken by 'Dr H' to another department – an army unit, very hush-hush. My work in future would be in this section, which was known as T.I.S. (Theatre Intelligence Service). Apparently the people in this department were attached to the War Office and had recently arrived to work with the 'brains' of the civilians in this new Ministry. My work was to translate the secret reports coming in from France, and to pick out items from these and file them; also to go through photographs and pictures and to establish whether they were true or false. Many of the reports were in dialect, but I found them quite easy to translate as I knew several of the French dialects. Most of the officers connected with this section were Engineers, and I learned that we were working on plans for the invasion of Europe. Security was very tight. You could not go in and out of the building without signing out and in again, even if you only crossed the road and remained within sight, and no headed paper was in use, just blank sheets.

I was very surprised to find how interesting the work was, and felt that here at last was something I could get my teeth into. I began to look forward to each day, with congenial companions and work which I knew was appreciated. The files were growing fast. I knew France so well that it was easy for me to judge the accuracy of reports.

Towards the end of February 1942, after Singapore had fallen, I found an envelope in my in-tray marked 'Top Secret'. I opened it and read 'Report to Storey's Gate this evening after six-thirty. A car will be waiting to take you there. When you arrive ask for Mr Rance. This is a confidential matter for your eyes alone.'

At 6.30 p.m. my telephone rang and I was informed that a car was at the entrance for me. I went down and signed out, to be ushered into a chauffeur-driven Daimler. As we left the building I naturally began to wonder where I was being taken. Where was Storey's Gate? Why all the mystery? I realised that we were driving towards Whitehall.

It was quite chilly and most of the passers-by hurrying along were in uniform. We met some of the 'Mobile Mollies' ready to take up their positions. These were small anti-aircraft guns brought in most evenings. I well remembered the first raids on London – the silence between the falling of the bombs and the sound of the bombers. I think the silence terrified many people. I doubt whether the Mollies could have done much harm to the German planes, but they made a great deal of noise, and their busy pop-pop seemed to give confidence to the people of London and the suburbs. They felt that something was being done.

As we neared Whitehall I thought to myself, 'So we are going to the War Office.' We turned off and stopped at an entrance to an obvious Ministry, but it was not the War Office that I knew. I noticed a pill-box manned by Home Guards at the corner. The entrance to the building was sandbagged. The chauffeur opened the door for me and said, 'I shall not be waiting, madam.' I thanked him and entered the building. There were many soldiers there. I noticed that they were Coldstream Guards and concluded that I was in another branch of the War Office. An officer approached me and I asked for Mr Rance. He nodded and went to a telephone. A few minutes later an elderly man in civilian dress approached. 'Good evening,' he said, 'I am Mr Rance.' I thought, 'Obviously a civil servant.'

George Rance was indeed a civil servant. He was in charge of Storey's Gate. It was said that before the war he had been in charge of all the 'Mrs Mops' of Whitehall. At Storey's Gate someone once remarked, 'Rance is the Skill of this place and Churchill is its Character.' Storey's Gate, called 'The Secret Place' by Winston Churchill but by others 'The Hole in the Ground' and by service people 'The Annexe' was a series of cellars forty feet under Ministry buildings with six acres of bomb-proof rooms. The War Cabinet met there. In fact it was the seat of war. The Map Room and the Operations Room showed exactly how the war was going. High personnel of Admiralty, Army and Air Force plotted the various operations. There were many coloured telephones giving direct contact with bases. When America came into the war a 'cubby hole' about twice the size of a telephone kiosk held the direct telephone line between Winston Churchill and President Roosevelt. This had a notice on it 'Keep Locked'. Of course I knew nothing of this at the time of my first visit, and nothing of George Rance. I said, 'I was told to report to you from the M.E.W.' He nodded and asked me to follow him, and I realised that we were on our way to the basement. We went along a corridor where there were several concrete blocks supporting the area. We neared a group of Marines, and there were also some civilians with them. The latter nodded to Mr Rance. We stopped at a door. Mr Rance knocked and a voice said, 'Come in.'

I think my heart missed a beat. That voice - it couldn't be! I must be dreaming. Why should *he* want to see *me*? Mr Rance opened the door and ushered me in. I thought my legs were going to give way, so I sat down hurriedly in a vacant chair. The door closed and I was alone with Winston Churchill.

I was conscious of the voice again, somewhat sarcastic: 'Do sit down.' I immediately stood up. An amused smile crossed his face and he motioned me into the chair again.

'I had to sit down, sir,' I apologised, 'because my legs were weak with shock. I had no idea I was to see *you*.'

He was sitting in the chair opposite mine studying me over the top of his spectacles and looking very casual and comfortable in a sort of battle-dress that reminded me of a baby's rompers. He needed comfort since he spent so much of his time in the Secret Place.

'I was given to understand,' he said drily, 'that you were in complete control of your nerves - at all times.'

As I recovered from my shock he explained why it was necessary to meet in this mysterious fashion. From now on I was to be a member of his Secret Circle, which had only twelve members. I was to be the only woman among them. We would not know one another or meet at any time. I was somewhat startled by this development as I had not foreseen a new career. 'I understand you fly,' he added.

'I have flown an aircraft, sir.'

'Are you correcting me?' he inquired.

I did not reply, though I was tempted to say, 'I thought perhaps you expected me to have wings!'

'Why did you learn ju-jitsu at the Sorbonne?'

I told him that some of the men students got fresh and I had to put them in their place. After I had thrown two of them downstairs they left me alone.

'I trust they weren't seriously injured?'

'Oh no,' I said, 'just badly bruised.'

He chuckled, and went on to ask me how I came to be familiar with the dialects of France, and various other questions which showed that the Powers that be had been busy with my background, and that Churchill had done his homework thoroughly.

'You seem to have a very quick brain,' he said. 'Almost as quick as my own.'

I could only murmur, 'Really, sir?'

'Whether you realise it or not,' he continued, 'you have many valuable assets. Your knowledge of France and French dialects, your retentive memory, your photographic mind, can all be used in the service of our country. You are naturally wondering how. We are shortly to be joined by a man who will explain everything to you. I won't tell you his name. We shall simply refer to him as The Major. And speaking of names' - he pinned me suddenly with a very bright blue stare - 'what are we to call you, eh? Initials J.B. ... h'm ... that would do, wouldn't it? Yes, we'll call you Jay Bee.'

There was a knock at the door. The Major had arrived. It was the man who had waited in my room at M.E.W. and whom I had snubbed for questioning me about my work. I did not move a muscle - I did not intend to be accused again of not having my nerves under control.

'You have already met the Major,' said Churchill. 'Do you remember him?'

'Should I, sir?' I asked innocently.

He laughed aloud and said, 'I knew we had made the right choice, Major.' Then he turned to me. 'Jay Bee,' he said gravely, 'you will have to give up your identity in the service of your country. All records of your association with F.A.N.Y. have been removed. You will live for the time being in a flat in Sloane Street. This means a complete break with friends and family; they must not under any circumstances know of your work. Just say you are on special work at M.E.W. requiring a change of address. Your social life will be nil. If you are asked out you can make excuses - or your cousin will impersonate you. Oh yes, we know all about your double. The Major will see her and brief her. You will not approach her yourself.'

The reason why I was not to see my family or friends was because sentiment sometimes overcomes reason and even sense of duty. If I was completely severed from them, my concentration would be entirely on my work in the Circle. Although I would be at the M.E.W. from time to time I must still avoid contact with anyone. My brothers were on active service and so was my husband, so there were no problems there. Indeed they were rather angry with me, because they thought I had chosen a 'cushy job' at the Ministry instead of doing something more worthwhile!

I asked why my cousin was to be used in my place - surely if I was not around I would not be asked out. He told me that it was necessary for me to be known to be in the country and working at the M.E.W. It would suit their purpose if I still worked there part-time, my cousin substituting for me when I had to be away. The Secret Circle was unorthodox, and unknown to everyone with the exception of Churchill, the Major and four others. If anyone ever found out about it and suggested that I was a member, it could be proved that I had been working continually at the M.E.W. My cousin would be trained to take my place there. She was not familiar with French dialects, but spoke French fluently and was a good actress. I had a feeling that she was going to enjoy the deception, as she had often made a date with a boy friend of mine and it was never found out. She could not, however, deceive my father, hard as she tried on many occasions. The officers I worked with in M.E.W. were very intelligent and I wondered how she would manage to deceive them. I imagined there would be someone there who was in on the secret, and would help her if necessary - perhaps one of the 'four others' whom Churchill had mentioned was in the M.E.W. - probably the Minister himself, who was a great friend of Churchill's.

I was told that when I had settled into the flat in Sloane Street I would meet a Major of the Royal Engineers who would escort me to and from Tempsford. I asked where Tempsford Aerodrome was. Churchill at once remarked, 'I prefer the word Airfield. Please use it in future.' He had some strong likes and dislikes about words, always preferring those of Anglo-Saxon origin. This airfield was a secret one between Bedford and Cambridge. I was to go to France in a Lysander aircraft piloted by a Fighter Pilot. I protested at this point that I would never be able to parachute, I was sure it would be the death of me. I was told to be quiet and listen. I would not be expected to parachute, I would be landed. I felt a great relief.

The Lysander was a wonderful versatile monoplane with a single 905 Bristol Mercury XII, 9 cylinder engine. Its range was roughly 600 miles and it had a maximum speed of 250 miles per hour. Its length was 30½ ft, with a width of 14½ ft, and a wing area of 260 sq. ft. The Lysander's 'ceiling' was 26,000 ft, but I learnt that we would fly fairly low.

I realised later how important this particular plane was for the work involved. The pilot seemed able to do as he pleased with it. I think its special wing flap made this possible, as it became airborne so easily that the pilot did not need to bother about wind direction. The Lysander is essentially a two-seater. Occasionally three and even four people had flown in one in an emergency, but no luggage was allowed when this happened, and of course the plane was no longer so manoeuvrable.

Before my interview with Churchill was over he again emphasised the need for secrecy. Few people, he explained, knew of the existence of the Circle, and the fewer the better. 'You may have to serve in this manner for two or three years,' he told me, 'depending on the length of hostilities. You can expect no medals or honours and your work will mean sacrifice. This is an unorthodox war, and the methods used in the Circle will be unorthodox. It will be a lonely life, but I think you will serve your country well.'

He explained that the S.O.E. was a saboteur force – one could say it was a subversive force – but the Secret Circle could well be termed a Reconnaissance unit, getting information to help to set up a Second Front for the liberation of Europe. I was glad that I was not a member of S.O.E. Their work involved destruction and possibly killing.

Churchill turned to the Major and asked him to take me to

Sloane Street and brief me further. He said goodnight to us both, and we left.

I still could not believe that I was not dreaming. I was in a trance, and it must have shown. When we reached the street I stood still and gulped in lungfuls of fresh air. The Major said, 'I think you could do with a drink.'

'I certainly could,' I said. 'I need a life-saver.'

We had drinks at the Ritz bar and then a meal. The Major seemed to be well known there. I was ready for that meal, and remember it to this day. We had mussels in parsley sauce, followed by an omelette and finished with a savoury toast. We drank a bottle of hock and talked about mundane things. Afterwards we walked to Sloane Street. I enjoyed the stroll through the quiet, dark streets.

We entered a large block of flats and I was introduced to the porter - but not by name. The Major explained that I would be using a flat there which I found was in the name of a Group Captain of the R.A.F. I wondered if he ever used it, or if it was just a 'front'. The porter seemed quite uninterested in me, only telling me that when I slept there I should put 'one lady' against the flat number on the record board. This was in case the building was hit in an air raid. I thought that if that happened the record board could well be destroyed; but why worry?

I inspected the flat. It was well furnished but small, with a tiny kitchen and bathroom and a shower. The kitchen was adaptable and was all electric. It had a cupboard well stocked with plenty of tinned fruits and meats. I told the Major I could always manage without meat, but I loved all kinds of fruit, and he said he would see that I had plenty. I think most of it came via the Americans. I said that I would arrange to move in within the next two days, as I had several matters to deal with.

Before retiring that night I went over the events of the day. In a few hours my life had been completely changed. I felt that I was ready-made for the work that lay ahead of me. I loved being alone, and it would not worry me to be anti-social. In fact, it seemed as if my whole life, from childhood on, had been a preparation for the task that had been allotted to me.

I went 'sick' for two days at the M.E.W. as I needed to gather my wits. Within four days I was established at the flat and awaited further developments.

3

Briefing and Training

Within a few days the Major was in touch with me. He asked me to go through my wardrobe, handbags, etc. to see if I had anything 'Made in England'. Actually I had lived in France for so long that all my possessions were made on the Continent - even powder compact, shoes, stockings, handkerchiefs and gloves. I could not remember having purchased anything in England for years.

The Major asked if I smoked. When I told him I did not, he said, 'You will have to carry cigarettes because you will have a lighter which will, on adjustment, become a compass.' I would be given a cigarette case made and sold in France. My watch was taken from me and I received in exchange one which could also be made into a compass. It was a Swiss make and the name was on the back. One agent selling the watch was in the Rue de Rivoli. No detail was overlooked. I must be French from top to toe.

It was arranged that my best cover would be to pose as a schoolteacher on supply, relieving others who might be sick, or where there was a temporary vacancy. I was told that the Germans did not appear to interfere with schools or brothels and did not search them unless they had specific information. I hoped that I would not be expected to take up residence in a brothel!

I learnt that the terms of the capitulation of France had been fairly generous on the part of the Germans. They were going to occupy the North of France. The rivers Cher and Loire and the Loire Valley were the demarcation line. The Channel and Atlantic coastlines were forbidden zones. People entering these areas would need a special pass from the Gestapo. The Frontier Zones were also made forbidden zones, and here again security was strict, workmen in these areas had to have the Gestapo stamp on their work papers. This showed two birds facing each other in a circle. I was to learn later that this stamp was referred to as 'the love birds', and I myself would be asking, 'Do you know anyone with love birds?'

The Midi and the South of France were Free Zones. The terms 'North', 'South' and 'Midi' do not denote strictly demarcated areas. As I shall often be using them, I shall explain here what I mean by them. We in Paris thought of them roughly like this: North of Tours was the 'North', south of Tours was the 'Midi', but the extreme south of France - that is, anywhere south of Toulouse and including the whole Mediterranean coastal area - we usually referred to as the 'South'.

Vichy, the base of the puppet French government, was in the Free Zone, but already in 1941 the Germans were beginning to occupy this so-called 'free' zone. Vichy is not far from Lyon, and this was an area I knew well. In fact I was very familiar with the Midi and the South and especially with the Basses-Pyrénées, having many British friends in the Pau district. I had spent my holidays from the convent and the Sorbonne on my father's estate between Nice and Grasse, which he sold just before the war. My knowledge of these parts was to prove of great use to me later.

I was to have two identities, one for the Occupied Zone and one for the Free Zone. False papers would be arranged. I learnt that Occupied Areas varied in the way they were governed by Military Commanders. Some were Nazi officers from the S.S. Others were professional soldiers who were not concerned with politics; they were merely concerned with duty as they saw it under Occupation. They were generals or colonels and treated the French people very well. Brittany had a Nazi Commander in charge. Paris and the North, as well as South Belgium, had a very lenient German professional soldier. This was General Falkenhausen, who was removed later as he was considered too kind. Normandy also had a professional soldier, 'Le Bosche', very charming to most of the people. He told them to carry on as usual; there would be no trouble unless they started it.

The Major explained that I would have to be very careful when I moved about freely from place to place. I was not afraid. I knew I would frequently face death, but I have always accepted that we all have to meet this stranger at some time. However, we may be able to defer the meeting. I hoped my philosophy would help me, and indeed it did. I had, and still have, a tremendous faith in God, and I had for years been able to meditate, and gained great comfort from this.

It was arranged that I should learn 'Soft-Karate', the killing art of the Samurai used by both the Chinese and Japanese. The milder form of 'Combat-Karate' is now taught. It is a mixture of

Judo, Kung Fu and Karate. The name 'soft' is deceptive, because this form entails really hard hand-chopping. I learnt the art from a Japanese expert. It was very painful at first and was mainly a question of breathing. The Japanese expert who taught me warned that I should not hold the 'lung position' longer than forty seconds; if I did not empty my lungs quickly I could very easily concuss my nervous system. I allowed myself thirty seconds to be on the safe side. Few people have mastered this form of karate. I told the Major that, although trained to kill with my hands, I would never do so. I was a doctor. I was prepared to put people out of action, but not to kill. He merely smiled and said, 'We shall see.'

I had always been very active. I had walked a great deal before the war, I rode, and was an accomplished high-jumper. I could climb a tree as well as any of my brothers.

The Major told me to look back and try to remember details of how the women of France behaved - in Brittany, in Normandy, in the large provincial cities and in the small villages. I must bear in mind always, he said, that the German S.S. and the Gestapo were very highly trained. They were professionals and I was an amateur. I would be up against an expert Secret Service, the Abwehr (equivalent to our M.I.5). When in France I must forget Britain and think and act like a Frenchwoman. This might be the most difficult task of all - to forget family, friends, security and all that made life pleasant.

It was emphasised that I must never carry firearms. I would be taught how to transmit and receive messages by radio. The codes would be changed often as they were secret ones, and they might be broken by experts on both sides in the war.

The Major explained that the minimum of time must be wasted between the arrival of the pick-up aircraft in France and the take-off. Also, I was to be taught how to drop out of a moving plane at four feet from the ground, as this might be necessary. I was taken to Lincolnshire to practise this. The plane was a Lysander and the pilot an expert. It was a nightmare.

I wore a padded suit to practise in, but I was not very successful in the eyes of the Major or the pilot. They thought I could easily injure myself seriously. I was certain that I would eventually break my neck, and told them so. It was decided to bring in someone to teach me how to fall. This proved to be a former circus clown. He taught me to wind myself into a ball - 'Head on tummy, knees drawn up, arms holding knees!' - these were the words I had coursing through my brain day and night.

After twenty-five falls I mastered it. I lost my front teeth, scarred my nose and upper lip slightly, but I mastered it - and when I finally fell out without a padded suit I was jubilant. I think I had reason enough to be pleased with myself. I was forty-one years of age, and the timing was split-second. I had always had a quick brain, but it seemed to act even more quickly at this period. I found myself counting time in seconds, not minutes. The tempo of life had quickened.

My teeth were replaced by a French dental surgeon. This was yet another safeguard; in the event of my capture there would be no British dental work to betray me. The Major did not miss a trick!

My lip soon healed, but left a scar which never entirely disappeared. This meant that when Jo and I were groomed to double for each other at the M.E.W., we both had to wear rather heavy lipstick, and heavy make-up to match. This did not worry Jo - she had always worn heavier make-up than I had. The only other marked difference was our hair. It was the same shade of dark brown, and we both wore it short. I wore mine parted in the middle, Jo at the side, but she also had a dead nerve which had caused a white streak in it - it was really rather becoming. I now acquired a similar white streak for use at the M.E.W., and had to remember to part my hair at the side.

Our likeness was now pronounced perfect. The streak was dyed when I went into France - each time - and then bleached again on return.

It was after 10 p.m. on a July night of 1942 when the Major and I arrived at the Secret Place. The Prime Minister greeted us, but did not seem his usual cheerful self. He asked the Major how I was getting on with my training, and the Major assured him that I had made very good progress and would be ready by the Autumn 'when you require her to go in'. Churchill turned to me and said he was very pleased to hear it, but in the meantime he wanted me to continue with my work at the M.E.W. It was a very important task, and my understanding of it was much appreciated. I wondered how he knew. There was much going on of which I was unaware. Perhaps it was better so!

He seemed deep in thought and I could not help thinking he was feeling the burden of office severely. It was especially heavy at this time and there was a lack of understanding on the part of many people. There had been demonstrations in Trafalgar Square and in the Albert Hall (including some Members of

Parliament) mainly Labour and Pacifists demanding more help to Russia in the way of equipment. To see and hear these people, one would have thought that Russia had come into the war specifically to help us. The truth was that the Russians had no choice but to fight or else surrender to Hitler. The Neutrality Pact Russia had signed with Germany in 1939 had been broken - undoubtedly much to their surprise.

Few people except those involved realised the difficulty of getting supplies to Russia. It was a nightmare journey round the North Cape to Murmansk, the only route other than a single track line through the Persian Highlands. Convoys were constantly attacked by U-boat packs, as well as aircraft and surface ships operating from Norway. A very high toll was being paid. Between April and June 1942 130,000 tons out of 200,000 tons of cargo were sunk by the enemy. Forty-nine ships went down and hundreds of seamen perished in the icy seas.

The pressure on the Prime Minister was enormous. He realised the suffering of the people of Russia and the effort being made, but he could not perform miracles. There were laden ships in British ports and supplies building up in America, all awaiting convoys. Appeals from President Roosevelt to get the supplies moving prompted Churchill to tell him that 'it was beyond his power to fulfil the requests as the British were fully extended'. Having said this, he did all that was possible to get the convoys moving. Only he could do this because of his courage, his faith, and above all his 'interference'. He was his own Minister of Defence because he did not trust others to keep him informed - for the same reason he set up the Secret Circle.

At the same time service chiefs were complaining at the loss of equipment which was being sent to Russia. They felt it would have been of greater use on our own fronts, especially the tanks. I heard some of these complaints at the M.E.W. I wanted to scream out in defence of Churchill, to tell them of his dedication and the weight of the burden he carried, one which they were not helping to ease, but I could not.

Sitting there in the Secret Place, seeing the lines of weariness and despondency on his face, I suddenly felt impelled to speak my thoughts aloud. I said that many of us knew just what he was trying to do, how helpless we felt, how I wished I could have lightened the burden he carried, if it were possible. The Major's expression showed surprise and almost fright at this outburst, and then relief when Churchill said, 'Thank you, Jay Bee. I thank God that I have a wonderful shoulder to weep on; that of my wife, my darling Clemmie.'

I felt he had conferred an honour on me by allowing me to share that brief moment of his intimate thoughts. I could only think, 'What a wonderful woman she must be, and what a blessing to us all that she is around when he needs her!' Even after all the years between then and now, I can still only wonder how he managed to carry the burden of leadership in these dark and difficult days, and on top of all this inspiring us with his faith in the British people. It was during these uneasy months in 1942 that on a visit to the North of England he spoke to hundreds of people in and outside Leeds Town Hall. His words were as follows:

'None of us is weary of the struggle, none of us is calling for favours; whatever we have got to take, we will take, and we will give it back in even greater abundance.'

He also found time to see the Minister of Food (Lord Woolton) and told him to let the confectioners have as much sugar as possible as he did not want the children to have to suffer too much from the shortage of sweets. And he made certain that the gun site personnel should have extra warm clothing for the winter months. The American and Canadian women sent over parcels of warm coats, many of them furlined and others completely made of fur. They were the envy of many Service people.

It was very early in the morning when the Major and I returned to my flat after this visit and I invited him in for a hot drink. He was in a talkative mood. We talked about my work and about the Secret Circle - the eleven men and myself - whom he referred to as his 'twelve disciples'. He told me that Churchill also had an Inner Circle, made up of his Parliamentary and Private Secretaries and his Service Aides. He placed tremendous reliance on these people, especially on General Ismay, his Defence Aide. The Prime Minister, the Major explained, did not want to involve his Inner Circle in something so unorthodox as the Secret Circle, and felt that the fewer people that were aware of it, the more likelihood it had of success.

It was at this time I learned that the Secret Circle had existed even before the war. Men in very important positions had been in touch with Churchill to tell him how worried they were about conditions in Defence. At least two of them continued to help during the war, in the Secret Circle. These were Professor Linderman and Group Captain Tor Andersom, the latter on Retirement Air Vice-Marshall.

The Major must have been very close to Churchill to be so completely trusted to deal with the members of the Circle. I never met the other men, although after the war I did learn that three of them died in Berlin, where they lived as Germans, and three others in Poland, where they worked in one of the rocket factories. All six were killed by Allied bombs. I have often wondered how their deaths were explained. Were they just written off as 'died on active service' or reported 'missing, believed dead'?

I felt at this stage that I too was carrying a burden with my knowledge of the Secret Circle which must never be revealed. About 5 a.m. the Major left. I wondered whether he had a home life, or whether he was one of those dedicated men who serve their country above personal comforts and desires. I was due to be at the Ministry at 10 a.m. so I decided not to go to bed, but to meditate.

I meditated a great deal after I left the convent where I was educated, and continued through the Twenties and Thirties. I considered that in many churches a man-made religion was being preached. I loved to go into a small church during the day and be alone. I had found that solitude was not loneliness - in fact it seemed a sort of communion. I had neither time nor mood to meditate during the recent hectic months of my training, but the urge to do so now was strong. As I had meditated over the years I had found that I could decide to wake at a certain time, and do so almost to the minute. The night was calm and quiet. I decided that I could meditate until 8.30 a.m.

As I drifted into space I prayed that the Allies would be given help to destroy the Nazi evil and that I should be given the strength to carry out successfully the tasks demanded of me.

I seemed to be above the Earth, and I was looking down on the British Isles. The seas around were very turbulent. I could not see any other country. Then I looked up and saw crowds of people - men, women, children, and many people in uniform. I heard my own voice saying 'Are you all dead? When did you die?' A young airman stepped forward, very fair, his eyes a vivid blue. He held a red rose in his hand which he slowly dropped. It seemed to grow larger until it covered the whole of Britain. I heard his voice saying, 'It does not matter *when* we died, what matters is *how* we died. All wars are futile. You must all declare peace in the world.'

Gradually the people faded away, and then I saw other

countries - France and Germany. There was a great deal of colour; over France it was red, and over Germany there were flames, as though it were on fire. I noticed that the sea was calmer and over the whole of Britain there was sunlight.

4

Poised for Action

In March 1942 we were again at Storey's Gate. Since we had last seen him, the Prime Minister had paid a visit to the East - Turkey etc. The Americans were anxious to get into Europe and had to be convinced that the time was not yet ripe. Admiral Mountbatten and General Brooke were sent later to America to persuade the President that it would be madness to try to liberate Europe until we had pushed the Germans and Italians out of the Middle East. Churchill had great faith in these two men and relied on their judgment. Many Service Chiefs resented his interference. They seemed to forget that he was Minister of Defence as well as Prime Minister and that nowadays the politician has the last word. General Brooke was reported to have said on one occasion, 'God knows what we shall do with his interference in everything we plan - but God knows what we should do without him!'

When George Rance escorted us to the Prime Minister I sensed an atmosphere of activity and alertness, despite his recent illness Churchill was in a fighting mood, so different from the last time we had met. He asked me how well I knew Paris, and whether I had friends among the Parisians. I told him I knew Paris and its suburbs very well but as to friends, I imagined many had left in 1940 when France capitulated; many, like the surgeon Thierry de Martel, had committed suicide rather than be arrested and used by the Germans.

Churchill shook his head sadly. 'How deeply I feel for the people of France,' he said. 'It is sometimes easier to resist than to try to live in peace under a military occupation. But of one thing I am sure. We shall liberate them as soon as it can be done.'

He asked if I thought it possible to spend a week in Paris 'looking around'. He wanted to know the attitude of the French to the Germans. The Parisians had now had military occupation for over two years while the Vichy government functioned in the Free Zone - although one wondered how free it in fact was.

Reports coming in from Paris were conflicting and it was difficult to get a true picture. I have felt since the war that much was kept from him, sometimes out of petty jealousy, and that this was why he found it necessary to do things in his own way. He himself rose above pettiness and small-mindedness. He told us that he found General de Gaulle very difficult to deal with. He had a chip on his shoulder, and seemed to think it his duty to be rude to the British.

Churchill wanted me to form a few groups in various parts of France, but he was especially anxious for first-hand information about Paris. I told him that Jacques, the concierge at the flats where I had lived before the war, was an extreme left wing trades unionist. I had always felt he might be a Communist. Before the war the movement was growing and the government was continually changing. It was very unstable, so it was no wonder that people had been influenced - the poor by the Left and the richer by right wing thinkers, many of whom were in sympathy with the National Socialism of Hitler. I had heard via friends that many Communists had been arrested before the war and at its outbreak. It was possible that Jacques had suffered this fate, but if he was still free and in Paris I was sure he would help me.

Jacques always seemed to imply that he owed me something for having given his wife medical aid. She had developed a cancer which became terminal, but we were able to prolong her life for two years - years which, Jacques said, were the happiest he had known, because he and his wife had been so close.

'Well, Major,' said Churchill, 'you are sure that Jay Bee is ready to undertake this assignment?'

'Quite sure, sir. She has passed every test without flinching. I think she has enormous courage. She has the coolest approach of any woman I know - and of most men. She will not fail.'

I felt very proud that they both put such faith in me.

I was told not to underestimate the Germans, especially the Gestapo. I said I was not afraid, as I could truly pass as a Frenchwoman. At that time I knew France better than I did England. The Major would give me all available information on which parts of Paris had been taken over by the Germans. He said some of de Gaulle's staff were in touch with people there and he would pick their brains.

'I shall soon be going to the Middle East,' Churchill told us. 'I want a change in the African Command. We need to clear the Germans out of Africa.' The Major asked whom he had in mind. He said the man he wanted did not get the support of the War

Cabinet, apart from General Brooke, and he was in a dilemma. I was sure I ought not to be present during this conversation. I had quite enough secrets to cope with and felt embarrassed, but when I moved to depart the Prime Minister motioned me to stay. I said that when I was troubled I had always prayed and meditated, and it had brought results. I knew that he too meditated. He turned to me in surprise and said, 'You are very observant. Most people imagine I just cat-nap.'

The Major and I returned to Sloane Street, where we talked until 4 a.m. He told me that on dangerous missions I would carry a capsule of cyanide and that the Prime Minister would decide when I should do so. I thought somewhat wryly that as far as I was concerned all missions would be dangerous. The capsule would have to be hidden, not carried in my handbag, but there would be time to think this over and decide where to hide it before a 'dangerous' assignment.

I would of course have to have French money. I told him I did not want to carry much of it, but he said we must provide for any contingency. When I left Paris in 1938 I had closed my bank account and had transferred some money to a solicitor friend who had a practice in Monte Carlo and Nice. I could always get money from him. The Major warned me to be very careful in my approach to him, but he relied on my judgment. He said that because of my photographic mind and retentive memory I would not need a camera or pen and paper. It would be much safer not to carry them. He only hoped I could bear the strain.

After he had left I went to bed for a few hours and then reported for duty at the M.E.W. We were piling up a great deal of information there. It was coming in from the various underground cells and had to be sorted out. The American Intelligence Officers who had recently joined us seemed to have little knowledge of Europe, but they were very enthusiastic and their energy was enormous. I began to like them as individuals. I thought General Eisenhower was a very charming man and at the same time I felt he was a great statesman rather than a great soldier. He had endless patience, particularly with General de Gaulle; whereas, whenever Churchill met the General, within ten minutes the air seemed to be sizzling with electricity.

At the end of August the Major told me that the Prime Minister was back from the Middle East and Russia, and early in September we were summoned to Storey's Gate. It was late, and the atmosphere was very pleasant and relaxed. I could always judge

Churchill's mood by the behaviour of the famous cigar. When he was feeling cheerful he smoked hardly at all, sometimes just holding a cigar in his hand and seemingly forgetting its existence. When he was angry or disturbed, on the other hand, he would puff at it furiously. I remember one occasion when he was on the hot line to the White House and things were evidently not going to his satisfaction, the 'cubby hole' was so full of smoke that he was almost invisible when he emerged.

On this occasion he looked tired, but not depressed, and after a few minutes he seemed to have shaken off the tiredness. The Major often said, 'He gets a second wind after 10 p.m.' We rightly assumed that his recent visits abroad had been successful. 'Our prayers have been answered,' he said. 'We have the finest strategist in charge of the Eighth Army. I only wish it could have been achieved under less tragic circumstances. But is the hand of Destiny.'

He was lost in thought for a moment and did not pursue the subject. He asked me if I was satisfied that I could get into Paris. I told him I was quite confident. I had no fear and would keep a cool head.

'But you must treat it as a dangerous assignment,' he urged. 'You must treat all entries into France as highly dangerous.'

I told him I had every intention of staying alive.

He nodded. 'It is right to be confident,' he said, 'but you will experience physical fear. Everyone at some time in life experiences physical fear. But it does not last. The real danger is mental fear. One must learn to overcome it.'

I wondered how many times he had faced fear himself - both mental and physical. He certainly understood its nature.

An amused look came into his eyes, as at some recollection. 'The Germans are funny people,' he said. 'Remember this, Jay Bee. They never believe the obvious. They always suspect there is a catch somewhere.'

These words, and the very tone in which he spoke them, impressed themselves on my mind, and later, in a dangerous moment, I had occasion to be glad of this.

'The Germans are machines,' he continued, 'but if you think machines can be broken, you should never forget that they can also crush you. Never take the Germans for granted, never underestimate them.'

As he was in a mood to talk, I asked him how he came to know so much about people, about human nature in general and individual and racial differences.

'I was not a good scholar,' he replied. 'I was not the happiest of schoolboys, but when I was a young soldier I read every book I could lay my hands on – the good, the bad and the indifferent. I learnt a great deal from my reading, but I believe I learnt even more from Stephen Jerome, my uncle. One could describe him as a "lovable scamp". He could charm any man or woman, and he used this talent frequently to help him in his many schemes for making money. He had an amazing knowledge of people and an uncanny gift of forecasting their reactions. To listen to him was a liberal education.'

He was smiling at his reminiscences, but his thoughts took a sudden change of direction and he turned abruptly to the Major. 'I want her to go into France next month. Please work it out.'

We said goodnight and walked to Sloane Street. It was a lovely, mild night of early autumn. The Major had left a bottle of hock at the flat when he called for me and we drank it with some Spam sandwiches. I was curious about Churchill's reference to destiny and tragic circumstances. The Major explained that the Prime Minister had always wanted General Montgomery to take over command of the Middle East under General Alexander. However, he was so often opposed by the Service Chiefs and others of the War Cabinet that he had suggested either General Gott or General Wilson, being sure that any suggestion coming from him would be turned down. To his surprise and dismay they had all, with the exception of General Brooke, supported the choice of General Gott. His bluff had failed.

Churchill had nothing against General Gott, but knew that he had gone through a gruelling time in the Middle East and was a very tired man. Gott was at that time resting at Beirut. He was told to report to General Alexander at Alexandria on August 7th, 1942, and flew with his staff in his transport plane to keep the appointment. They took the Burg-el-Arab-Heliopolis route, which was considered so safe that the Prime Minister had been flown over it without escort planes. The slow transport was on its way when a lone German plane appeared, apparently driven from high altitude to low and possibly on its way to its base. The pilot spotted the transport plane and shot it down in flames. All the occupants were killed. A truly ghastly end for a devoted General and his staff.

General Brooke was reported to have said after the tragedy that General Gott, though indeed very tired, being the man he was would not give in. He was a soldier who put his country first. Had he taken up the command in his then state of health the outcome might have been very different.

The command was given to General Montgomery and Churchill had his wish. He had obtained the man he felt was best suited to deal with the Middle East campaign. He considered that General Montgomery was a 'showman' and that he would inspire the troops and his officers with his ambition and his 'sheer cheek'. And this he did. From the moment he took over command he went on the attack and fought through to victory, helped by the Americans when they caught up with each other.

The Major said Churchill had a great ability to choose the right people when he was in a tight corner. He chose Lord Mountbatten to be Chief of Combined Operations and later for Supreme Command Far East, because he was a good mixer. The Americans liked him, his adventurous spirit and brilliant brain were used in the service of his country. Churchill admired General Brooke. He had a deeply spiritual character and was a man of great honour. I wonder sometimes if these three men realised how much he relied on them.

The Major told me that the visit to Stalin had also been a success, but only after both men had hurled insults at each other, and Churchill had won the battle of words. Each man respected the other afterwards, and it was rumoured that the only ally that Stalin respected was our Prime Minister. The latter did not try to be friendly, but treated him as an ally, whilst remembering that he had come to power through blood and torture. It was often reported that President Roosevelt tried very hard to be on really friendly terms with Stalin, but never quite succeeded. Stalin was an enigma. His only friend was himself. He had the talent for bargaining that most Asians possess - he took, but gave little in return.

I found the Major a very interesting and informative person, and wondered what his true relationship with the Prime Minister was. Although he was always known as the Major I felt that he was undoubtedly of higher rank. I sometimes had an urge to pinch him to see whether he was real and human, but I resisted the temptation. My convent training must have had some influence on my natural unruliness!

On our next visit to Storey's Gate the atmosphere was electric. I heard afterwards that there had been a shouting match amongst the War Cabinet. Many of them, in particular Sir Stafford Cripps, had tried to put pressure on the Prime Minister, but he had shouted them all down. One of the Marines on guard in the corridor was heard to comment: 'If old Hitler could hear him he'd belt up and run.'

Some of this electricity still crackled in the air when we arrived, but before Churchill had time to deal with us his telephone rang, and when he had answered it he asked us to leave the room and wait in the corridor. We did so, and saw several men walking towards the Prime Minister's room, among them King George VI. I heard the King say, 'Hullo, Winnie, how are things going?' and then the door closed. The other men went into the Map Room.

In later months I was to see the King visit the Prime Minister on many occasions. They had a great deal in common - the love for the British people and their way of life. Not enough appreciation was ever given to this fine King. When he could not sleep because he was worrying about his people and the war, he would walk across the park to Storey's Gate. He was a sensitive, spiritual man, upset at the deaths of young service men and women and at the deaths of civilians in this evil war. He was a king who really served his people. He believed in the power of prayer and in National Days of Prayer because he was so aware of that power. He stayed in London with his people who were for a time the centre of Hitler's attacks. To me the greatest and most simple tribute is that made by Lord Halifax. This is a plaque at Garrowby in Yorkshire and it reads: *To the Glory of God and in memory of George, King, servant of the people, 1895-1952.* He left us the legacy of a fine family to carry on the monarchy and the sacrifice it has to make. I doubt if we fully realise that, whilst we, the people, are so free under our laws, our 'Royals' are never 'truly free'.

After the King had left we rejoined the Prime Minister and I was told that I would be going into France within a few days. I was to get to Paris and try to obtain a true picture of conditions there. My name in the Occupied Zone would be Yvonne Millescamp. My identity card was a forgery, but an excellent one. My fingerprints would be taken before its completion, and on it I would be described as a schoolteacher.

Winston Churchill wished me a safe journey and a successful mission. The dream had become reality. I was on my way.

5

Blind Assignment

Two days later I had a visitor. It was the major of the Royal Engineers who was to accompany me to the airfield and meet me on my return. He asked me to be ready the following evening and explained that I was going in 'blind' - which meant that I would arrive in France on my own and would have no help from others. One could not foresee the hazards that might arise; hence the term 'blind'.

I went through everything that I was to take with me - just a small case with underwear and a change of dress. It was late evening when the R.E. major called alone. I confess I was disappointed; I had expected the 'Major' would be with him. We drove from Sloane Street and headed north to Tempsford, where we had to wait a while. Then, to my relief, the 'Major' arrived. He gave me French money, identity card etc. and went over the briefing again. I felt quite calm, but I think the Major was uneasy. We had an excellent and plentiful meal of bacon and eggs, and I couldn't help feeling that this was the proverbial 'last meal'! I was introduced to the pilot as 'your passenger'. He was not the pilot with whom I had practised 'falling out', and I had been told not to hold a conversation with him.

Both majors stood by as I climbed into the Lysander and took my seat beside the pilot. They looked very serious, but when I smiled and waved to them I was given a thumbs up sign and the Lysander took off. The pilot's first words were, 'It's going to be a bit tricky.' I didn't ask which particular part he was thinking of. After a short flight we landed and I realised we were still in England. The pilot remained in his seat, and so did I. I presumed we were taking on more fuel. The clouds passed over the moon and as they cleared we took off again. As we flew low over the sea, the pilot remarked, 'Actually, low flying is against R.A.F. orders because of shipping.' Evidently the Major's orders took precedence over any others, and the responsibility was his.

I began to feel the thrill of flying again. It is a wonderful feeling in a small plane; there is never the same sensation of freedom in a large one. I envy birds having this freedom of flight. How wonderful if I could have gone on and on into the unknown, away from all the petty troubles and all the wickedness of man ... I pulled myself together. This was pure selfishness. I had a job to do and ought to be concentrating on it. I kept saying to myself, 'I am now French. I must forget England. I am French, French ...'

As we neared the French coast I saw guns in action quite clearly, but we were not hit. The pilot seemed to glide at times. He certainly had complete control of the Lysander. We were following a railway; it shone up through the semi-darkness like ruled silver lines. The river we followed later also gleamed like a twisted silver ribbon, and I felt a long way from war and destruction. We flew on and on and then, 'Get ready!' from the pilot. The plane glided down and then came the command 'Out!' Thank goodness the wheels were down; I did not have to fall out.

Within seconds the engine roared and he was off. I was sitting on the ground and I continued to sit. It seemed ages, but in reality it was minutes only. I gathered my thoughts and myself together, picked up my overnight case and left the field. I would be back here in a week's time - with luck. I looked at my watch. The time was 4 a.m.

I had always boasted that I had never felt lonely in my life, but now it seemed to me that I was the only person left in the world. I was in enemy-occupied country. I know no lonelier feeling.

As soon as I got moving, I quickly recovered. I had studied the area well from maps and photographs and knew the details of the route I was to take. I found the main highway to Tours without difficulty. The field where I had landed was heavy with dew, and for no logical reason I removed my shoes when I reached the main road and cleaned them carefully, wiping them with grass and then with a tissue. I heard my own voice saying, 'Idiot, who is going to care whether your shoes are clean or not?' I had spoken aloud - a reaction, I suppose. This would not do. As I walked on towards Tours I was surprised that I did not meet any traffic, possibly because I followed the road inland for a while. I saw signs of war. Some fierce fighting must have taken place, or perhaps the destruction was the result of German bombing. It had been reported that German fighters and bombers had blitzed the people leaving for the South after the capitulation of France. Hundreds were killed.

Tours lies between the rivers Cher and Loire, and as I approached it I saw that much of the town had been destroyed. I could not help thinking of the lovely châteaux in this area and wondering whether they too had suffered. I am glad to say that since the war Tours has been replanned and rebuilt, and is still the centre of really beautiful country.

When I arrived in the town I noticed Vichy policemen and many German soldiers. Everything seemed normal and casual. I made my way to the station, where groups of people, mainly elderly, were waiting, and among them were the distinctive uniforms of German soldiers and the S.S., but to my relief I saw no Gestapo.

On my visits to Germany before the war I had seen the growth of the Gestapo and I knew the uniforms well. The Himmler S.S. and the Waffen S.S. had different insignia, and the favoured Gestapo, the killers, had the honour of wearing a death's head signet ring, which it was said they never took off. They also had a dagger in the front buckle of their belts. I was to see later on what this blade could do.

I bought a ticket for Paris. No questions were asked, and thirty minutes later I entered a compartment with three other passengers in it. We nodded to one another and I took a seat by the door and pulled out a book of poems I had with me. The compartment began to fill up, and after a short time a Gestapo officer - the first I had seen since leaving Paris in 1938 - appeared in the doorway, looked us over, then came and stood in front of me and said in excellent French, 'Show your feet.'

I have a sense of the ridiculous, and my immediate reaction was to giggle. He glared at me, and in a few terse sentences I was told exactly what happened to people who laughed at Gestapo officers. I apologised, and explained that I was not laughing at him, but at his request. Did he really want to see my feet?

He stared hard at me. 'Your shoes, of course.'

I took them off and handed them to him. He scraped the sole with a small file and then scraped between the uppers and soles and under the heel. He seemed satisfied and returned them. He did not ask for my papers, but went on to the other passengers and carried out the same procedure. Two men passengers were asked for their papers, which were scrutinised and then returned to them. I looked out of the window and saw several other officers, so apparently all compartments had been checked.

Shortly afterwards the train moved off, and the passengers

breathed a sigh of relief. I asked the man sitting next to me why
they examined our shoes but did not seem concerned with identity
cards. He said they were looking for mud. I looked surprised, and
he explained, 'In the area of the river Cher it is muddy. If you had
had mud on your shoes you would have been interrogated, as
people sometimes cross over the Cher or the Loire from the Free
Zone without passes.'

I reflected on my instinctive action of cleaning my shoes when I
reached the road. The landing ground was near the river; I felt I
had been helped in some way, and it gave me confidence.

As we travelled I noticed the scars of war and began to wonder
what state I should find Paris in. It had been declared an 'open
city' on capitulation, so should have been safe from bombing. We
arrived half an hour late; apparently this was not unusual. There
were many people on the station, including Germans in uniform,
but we passed through the ticket barrier without trouble. I was in
Paris - in enemy-occupied Paris - and on my own for six days.

As I walked from the station I had a strange sense of unreality. I
had expected to find Paris profoundly changed, and instead it
seemed quite normal. I found myself resenting this normality. It
was all wrong. Paris had endured a dignified capitulation in 1940,
and now she had accepted German occupation and appeared to be
living a normal life. And then I thought, 'Why not? Life must go
on. Human beings are very adaptable, or they would not survive.'

I made my way to the Place de l'Etoile. I do not like its new
name, Place Charles de Gaulle. When I think of Paris, it is the
'Place de l'Etoile' that I remember. Paris, with the twelve avenues
leading from this centre on to boulevards and other avenues
which cross one another, all having their own beauty and their
own character; and encircling the city are the *portes*, the gates of
Paris. It is indeed a lovely city.

As I looked at the great Arc de Triomphe, under which lies the
grave of the Unknown Soldier, I noticed the four German flags,
the hated swastika, and I realised that Paris was not, after all,
normal. Its atmosphere was tainted. I turned away in disgust.

I saw two light tanks patrolling, escorting some German cars,
and I had the odd feeling that I was not on the ground; I seemed to
be at a height, looking down at them. I passed the 'Select Bar'
which was known as a 'male slave market'. This was a place where
one could pick up a male prostitute. There was a notice outside in
French and German, 'Out of bounds to the Army', but I noticed
some S.S. troops going in. Many S.S. men had the reputation of

being homosexuals, and they did not come under the orders of the
Wehrmacht (German Army).

I walked past Maxim's. It was crowded. Obviously there were
still plenty of people with money to spend. The theatres were
open and in full production. I began to feel that this was not the
Paris I used to know. Where was the Paris of Voltaire? Where were
the French who believed in the pursuit of Glory? Had the
Mediterranean world surrendered to the Nordic and Atlantic
nations? Had they surrendered themselves to decadence?

No, Paris must not lose her Parisians! We must not let them die
out or become zombies, we must bring them to life again. For the
first time I understood how General de Gaulle felt about Paris;
how Napoleon and Joan of Arc had felt.

I went along the Avenue de la Grande Armée where in pre-war
days I used to frequent a small café. I had been very friendly with
the owner and his wife, Boris and Janine; they had always
produced some lovely meals for me, at very reasonable prices. I
had said goodbye to them in 1938, telling them I was going to
England. I decided that it would be safe to visit them - if they were
still there. There were several German soldiers in the café,
drinking, but luckily no officers. Boris was standing behind the
counter, and if he felt any surprise on seeing me he was careful not
to show it. I ordered a coffee and he brought it to the table. I asked
him if he had a telephone, and might I use it. I knew that it was
not in the café itself, but in their own quarters at the back. He said
certainly Madame could use it, he would show me where it was. I
followed him, and as soon as we were out of hearing and sight of
the soldiers we stopped. Boris threw his arms round me in a bear's
hug and said, 'You come from the Moon? You come to help us?'

Janine appeared, her eyes round with amazement. I put my
fingers to my lips, and she understood. Boris went back into the
bar and I whispered to Janine that I would return later if she
would let me in at the back door. She nodded and I went back into
the café. I drank my coffee and asked Boris what I owed for the
telephone (which I had not used); all this to impress the soldiers if
they were observing. When I had paid for the coffee and telephone
I left, went round to the back door and found Janine
weeping - tears of joy, she said.

She began to tell me about the Occupation. It was not too bad at
first; Fauenhauser, a German who was not a Nazi, had been in
charge, but now the Gestapo were in power and things were
changing. People had fled from Paris in June 1940. Many had

committed suicide, many had died on the way south, but after a month or so people began to flock back. There were a lot of Secret Police in Paris; their Headquarters were on the Left Bank. I think she was referring to the Abwehr, the equivalent of our M.I.5.

Presently Boris joined us, the soldiers having left, and Janine made coffee. I asked her if she could get plenty and she said yes, through the Black Market. Boris remarked that if you had money you could get anything - except tea. After chatting about old times I told them I had not returned to England in 1938 as I had intended, but had gone to the Riviera to stay with my father. We were in the Free Zone there, and I was working with Resistance groups. I wanted to get in touch with some in Paris, if there were any.

Boris did not know of any such groups, but was expecting some of his regular customers, many of whom operated the Black Market, especially in gold. People were trying to buy gold Louis and prices were very high. Both the Germans and the Vichy government were trying to get their hands on some. I asked what the police were doing about it. Boris laughed. 'They close their eyes. They know well enough what is happening. What better place to have gold than amongst the French people? The Germans would take it from the banks.'

I told Boris I wanted to get in touch with the concierge at the flats on the Ile St Louis where I had lived up to 1938. He telephoned for me and found Jacques there, but he would not believe that I was in Paris until he heard my voice. 'Wait there,' he said, 'I'll come for you as soon as I can.' Two hours later he was with me. I told him the same story - that I had not gone to England after all, but to the Riviera. He said he would take me back to the flats with him, as he had much to tell me, and after more tears and hugs I left Boris and Janine with the promise that I would see them again.

6

Mission Accomplished

When we left the café I asked Jacques if we had time to walk to the Ile St Louis, as I wanted to see as much as possible on the way. We talked as we strolled through the streets, being careful not to be overheard. Jacques confirmed that in 1940 the military occupation had been under a non-Nazi, General Fauenhauser, who had asked the Parisians not to resist, as he wanted to avoid any clash with the Gestapo. There had still been French Jews in Paris, trying to leave, and the General was sympathetic. Their homes were of course commandeered when they left, but they were allowed to take their jewels and movable articles with them and go south to the Free Zone. Many of them managed to escape with much of their movable wealth, but they had to pay an exorbitant price to the Black Market which ran traffic from the Occupied to the Free Zone.

I asked about the position of the Germans in Paris at the moment. He told me things had changed somewhat because the Abwehr had a large number of agents established on the Left Bank. The power there was in the hands of one Sergeant Bleicher, despised by the Military and hated by everyone else. Before his arrival in Paris, when the Army arrested a Resistance member there was no publicity. His clothes were returned to the members of his family, and they knew by this that he was dead. But under the Sergeant conditions were changed. He believed in torture and some very terrible stories were told. Jacques said the Sergeant boasted that he could 'smell an agent'.

I commented that I had expected to see more flags - Hitler loved a display of them. Jacques explained that many had been destroyèd by the Resistance - they felt that they were at least hitting back in some way. Apparently the Germans were slow to replace them; flags must be in short supply.

As we walked towards the Place de la Concorde - which I have always loved - I asked if the Germans had taken any of the

treasures of Paris. Most, he said, had been stored away from Paris.
The Germans had established an Inspector of Arts for the
Occupied Zone, who was also Chief Director of the Louvre (now
empty). This man was Count von Metterlinck, and apparently he
was quite genuine in his appreciation of art, especially paintings.
When he heard that troops were occupying Monet's house in
Giverny he sent a letter in his own hand-writing forbidding any
further occupancy by the troops, and they left without disturbing
Monet's paintings, some of which were still there.

Most of the Paris homes of the very wealthy Jews had been taken
over by Germans, and I asked Jacques if he knew what had
happened to the château outside Paris which the French
Rothschilds had given over for the benefit of Jewish orphans
expelled from Germany before the war. About forty of these
children lived there and the Rothschilds had provided nurses and
teachers and the funds with which to run the place. The
Rothschilds had been stripped of their possessions and their
French nationality and forced to leave Paris. The Germans took
over the château but some American Quakers managed to get the
children out of France to the United States to become American
citizens. I felt very relieved on hearing this and silently blessed
those Quakers.

We had now reached the Place de la Concorde and sat down for
a while. It is an impressive square, reputed to be the largest in the
world. To the north east lies the Rue de Rivoli, one of the best
shopping centres of Paris. The square has many lovely statues and
it is full of history.

Jacques pointed out several civilians. He said, 'All those men
are in the Black Market. They charge very heavily to get people
into the Free Zone; they are the people who traffic in gold and
jewels - human leeches.' He told me the Germans had taken over
all the gold in the banks in 1940, but many people had foreseen
this and withdrawn their gold. The Vichy government was trying
to buy gold and conceal it for future use. Dutch, Swiss and Belgian
stockbrokers had been in Paris buying up all they could. This
confirmed what Boris had told me. There was a Russian on the
Left Bank who secretly melted gold coins into small ingots the
size of a visiting card. They were easy to conceal and people with
permits to enter the Free Zone were used to take the gold across.

I inquired whether Hitler ever visited Paris, and Jacques said,
'Yes, incognito, also once publicly, when he made a dramatic
gesture to the Parisians by restoring to France the ashes of the

Duke of Reichstadt so that they should be placed in the Invalides near the remains of his father, the Emperor. The Parisians were not impressed. They chanted, 'We need coal, and they send us ashes!'

We went on our way towards the Ile St Louis, walking along some of the streets I knew so well. I realised again how beautiful Paris was and how right it had been to declare it an 'open city'. What a loss it would have been to Europe if all those lovely buildings had been destroyed. It was said before the war, 'Paris is the most beautiful city in Europe; Rome comes next to it; London is chaotic and New York systematic.' I cannot help feeling this is a fairly good summing up.

I had in the past always tried to view Paris as a tourist and not as a resident, and this view helped me to understand Paris and the Parisians. All French people love the soil of France, and I was very much aware of their attitudes. Frenchwomen like security and always dress to please their men. They love family life, but when they love they do so not because of a marriage contract but because they are hot-blooded and in love with love. Living in Paris and in other parts of France I learnt their way of life. French women will fight like vixens to defend their homes and the security of family life. There is little servility amongst the French, although there are social classes which move in their own distinct worlds. The worker of France has always felt, since the Revolution, on equal terms with his employer. I felt it was going to be very difficult for the Germans to deal with this traditional attitude.

These thoughts were crowding through my mind as we walked. When we arrived at the Ile St Louis it was a joy and a relief to see the Seine; it looked so peaceful. I did not notice many Germans, but Jacques pointed out several civilians whom he recognised as Germans. He was a mine of useful information. I had been very lucky in my choice of 'contact'.

The Ile de la Cité and the Ile St Louis are the islands on the Seine linked together. The former is the larger of the two and its main attraction is the great cathedral of Notre Dame. This beautiful building has witnessed many historical events in its time, but I cannot help feeling that the greatest of all took place on August 26th 1944, when General de Gaulle headed the Victory March to the cathedral to celebrate the Liberation of Paris from Nazi German control. The German General von Choltitz had surrendered the previous day to the leader of French Resistance. Had this General followed Hitler's command to 'Defend or destroy Paris stone by stone' it would have been a terrible disaster. He was not a Nazi and he disobeyed Hitler. I think the individual honour of the Paris Liberation lies with this man.

As I crossed the St Louis Bridge to the Ile St Louis I felt once more the tranquillity of its streets and houses. They are mostly seventeenth century, mellow with age, but one chose to live there not because of the beauty but because of the 'aloofness' from the hub of Paris. In fact I had often heard people on the Island say, 'I am going into Paris to do some shopping'. It was strange, this feeling; one was in the heart of Paris, yet one seemed right outside it.

It was lovely to be back in the past again - so much had happened to me since 1938, and although it was now only four years later it seemed an age. I asked Jacques if there were many Germans on the Ile. I was surprised to learn that General Rommel had taken over the building next to the flats; he used it occasionally when on leave, and some of his staff did also. He came very quietly and did not mix with the Nazi Germans in Paris. He seemed to avoid contact with anyone, as though he wished to be alone. I was not surprised, as I was sure Rommel despised the Hitler regime, but he was a professional soldier and undoubtedly loved his country, and so remained in the army.

The building in which I had an apartment was converted many years ago. It had been an hotel but few remembered it as such. Jacques said the Germans had inspected the apartments in 1940. He had told them I had left in 1937, and as I had a lease which had several years to run I had asked him to let the flat. He gave the name of his girl friend as the tenant. The Germans were not interested in living on the Ile. The Luxemburg and more luxurious houses elsewhere in Paris had been taken over by them. Goering and his staff had apartments in the Luxemburg, and soldiers were billeted in various suburbs of Paris. The S.S. regiments were right in the centre of Paris. There were many Frenchmen in the Waffen S.S. and they felt at home in the city.

Jacques introduced me to his girl friend Marie, who was a Parisian, about forty years of age, and worked in a post and telegraph office. I asked Jacques why he did not marry again. 'Not during the war,' he told me. 'After perhaps - if we survive.'

It was this remark that finally convinced me he was in the Resistance. I asked him if he was still interested in Communism and he seemed surprised that I knew. I explained that I had no interest in politics, but had heard in the South of France that many Communists had formed groups of Resistance and could be trusted. He said they were all Frenchmen with a love of France; they were not like Russian Communists. I could understand this. France had been unstable in her governments for so long that many people felt the only solution was Communism. Most of them, to my mind, were extreme left-wing trades unionists. I told Jacques so, and he seemed relieved that I did not object to his opinions. Marie remarked, 'You English are strange people, but you are very fair and just.'

I told Jacques I wanted to see as much of Paris as possible in a week, and I would like to stay at the flat. This was arranged. I explained that my *nom de guerre* was French and showed him my papers, ration books etc. He thought they were a good forgery and merely remarked, 'You will need a work paper with an address on it. I will get one for you with this address. I have connections who can do it.' I did not tell him that I had in my head another address in Paris - that of a 'safe house'.

Jacques and Marie promised to help me to get any information I wanted about Paris. We would go out together as if we were just friends enjoying ourselves. As I looked about me I came to the conclusion that there were five kinds of people here: some accepted and collaborated with the Germans; some accepted and did nothing; some behaved like ostriches and said to themselves, 'We must be patient and wait, the British are bound to win. They always do.' Others resisted as much as they could in secret; while others again openly studied the Germans and their New Order in the hope of breaking them. These last, I feared, might prove dangerous to the French as well as to the Germans.

I asked Jacques about Resistance in the Midi. He said he worked with people in Paris who were in touch with Resistance in Normandy and the Lyon area. They were Maquis, mostly from peasant and workers' associations, they did not work with any other organisation; they were mostly like himself - Communists but French patriots. After talking about the work I was doing in the South - I dared not confide my real work to him, it was better to trust no one further than necessary - Jacques agreed to give me the name and address of a contact in Normandy. He lived in the Caen district and worked on the railways.

I learned a great deal from this visit. Jacques was in touch with a great number of people in the Resistance, but they worked independently. He seemed to have contacts in all the main stations who could help with tickets. Railway and post and telegraph personnel were willing to assist in any way they could. One could visualise the havoc these people could cause if they were properly organised.

When my time was up I left my extra clothes at the flat so that I would not have to carry them back when I returned to Paris. Jacques told me that if I could return in about a month he would be able to furnish the names and addresses I needed in Normandy and Lyon. I did not of course mention England, I said I was returning to the South. He did not ask me how I travelled from the Free Zone to the Occupied Zone to reach Paris. On reflection later, I think he probably suspected the truth. Before leaving I had a celebration meal with Boris and Janine - a large plate of hors d'oeuvres variés with some of Janine's home-made rolls, made with egg, they were delicious.

I took the Metro to the station this time, as there was a stop for the Gare d'Austerlitz. There were several Germans travelling, but I kept my nose in a book and avoided looking at them. The journey to Tours was uneventful - it seemed almost too easy. From Tours I set off to make my rendezvous with the Lysander which would, I hoped, pick me up.

As well as the uncomfortable 'fall-outs' I had practised 'pick-ups' in Lincolnshire, and I thought they were dreadful. The R.A.F. insisted that wind direction was always marked with flares for the 'down wind' and 'up wind'. This was workable when one had help, but when one was alone it was difficult. I thought I would never master it in the time allowed and as I would be on my own the Major agreed with me. We practised without wind direction. I signalled with a torch, using a different code of flashes each time. The pilot would come in at 300 feet, and if he did not see my signal, he would circle and come in again. It worked well, and the operation took less than eight minutes once the plane had landed. I am sure the Lysander was the only plane that could achieve this. These planes became as important to our V.I.P. agents as the Jeep became to the Americans. We of course had expert pilots - our young fighter pilots had tremendous ability with Lysanders. Later on, when I had 'groups' to work with me, pick-ups became much easier.

All went well on this occasion; the Lysander came in quietly and in less than five minutes I was in the plane. I felt very happy that on my first assignment, a 'blind' one, everything had gone so smoothly and my mission had been successful. I would not have been quite so happy on the return flight if I had known that some of Goering's crack fighter pilots were billeted in the Tours area. Fortunately I learnt this only later.

The R.E. major was waiting for me at Tempsford with a flask of tea, which I enjoyed on the way to London. We hardly exchanged a word during the journey. I was taken to the Sloane Street flat and told to remain there until I was contacted.

I could not help a certain feeling of anti-climax about my triumphant return. There had been no excitement, no congratulation on my safe arrival. This was just an ordinary occasion and I realised that I would have to accept the fact and get used to it. Perhaps after all a flask of tea is sweeter than words of praise!

7

Allies, Enemies and Traitors

The Major's greeting when he appeared at the flat next day was, 'You're looking fine, Jay Bee. Did you enjoy yourself in Paris?' That was not an easy question to answer. I said, 'I don't know. I experienced regret, surprise, disgust, sorrow and a certain pleasure in finding that Paris was still alive, but it was not the Paris I used to know.'

I told him I had contacted Jacques with success, and all that had passed between us. He was obviously pleased, and said we would be visiting Storey's Gate very soon. Meanwhile I was to relax and wait, not go to the M.E.W. until he told me to. The following evening we were at Storey's Gate, and I went over all my experiences and impressions again for the Prime Minister. He was delighted with my report and asked a lot of questions. He said I must certainly return to keep in touch with Jacques and get the names of the men I could contact to form groups.

It was morning before we were back at the flat. The Major seemed to have a great deal on his mind. He did not stay, but said I could report to the M.E.W. next day.

Two days later he phoned me to meet him at the Mayfair Hotel, where we had dinner before returning to the flat for discussion. He wondered whether it might be possible to build an escape route from Paris right through France to the Basses-Pyrénées - the final town to be Tarbes. 'I can try', I said. 'Who would use it?' 'V.I.P.s only.' he replied.

He agreed that in future the Ile St Louis address of my flat should be used on all my papers; at least I had an ally there. The 'safe house' would be used only in an emergency. But before I went back to Paris I was to go to Normandy to photograph certain places in my mind. I would be given only two clear days and must then return to England, again by Lysander.

The Province of Normandy is very beautiful, especially in peace time. It has a mild climate where one can see the wonderful camellias, magnolias and fruit trees in abundance; good farm land, fat cattle and high-grade dairy produce. It has lakes, small rivers, and woodland, and is famous for its anemones and its calvados (apple brandy). In wartime, however, Normandy was a serious liability because of its geographic position. The Normans are a tough people, a toughness inherited from their ancestors, the Vikings. It was one of the descendants of these fighters who did what Napoleon and Hitler would have loved to have done – conquered England. He was William the Bastard, afterwards known as William the Conqueror.

The people I was to contact lived near Evreux. This was a lovely city before the war and on my arrival I was appalled by the damage done by the Germans. The cathedral had been hit and many streets completely destroyed. I made my way to the hamlet where the Major's friends lived. This was farming land, but a great deal of it showed signs of battle. The friends gave me a warm welcome and said the description the Major had given of me was most accurate.

I told them I had only two days to visit certain places; the farmer said it would be easy as he had permits to visit markets and to move about. They told me the Military Commander, Le Bosche, was not a Nazi, in fact he seemed to be very popular with the people of Normandy, as he left them alone. When the Germans arrived in Normandy, the Commander decided that he would make his headquarters at Bayeux. The sub-prefect called Pierre Rochat was reported to have asked him whether he would be confiscating their Treasury amounting to 5,000,000 francs. 'Le Bosche' replied 'What would I do with five million francs? Just give me a hotel for myself and my officers and a brothel for our use. Billet my men; do not make trouble or resist. I shall not interfere if you behave yourselves. We do not want Gestapo here.' He was based in Bayeux, and seldom moved out of it. The farmer said he had more trouble with the Vichy Police than with the Germans.

I liked these friends very much and they fed me royally – I even had the far-famed chicken and duck pie. They were gentlefolk in their sixties. Most of the workers were elderly too. The young and able-bodied had to work for the Germans. The farmer was a tremendous help to me; he said he would do anything to help England. When my brief visit was over and my assignment successfully carried out, he drove me part of the way to my rendezvous with the Lysander. I went on to a certain point by bus, then walked until I reached the pick-up field.

It was quite dark now. I hoped there would be moonlight later, for the landing. I had to wait for some time, but I was not a bit worried, as I knew I had friends in the area. It was a very warm feeling. At last I heard the Lysander, and when it landed I ran towards it, and less than eight minutes later we were in the air. I felt I was becoming expert at signalling a plane.

The Major was already at the Sloane Street flat when I arrived and he asked me to describe everything I had seen. I closed my eyes and could see a clear picture of all the details I had been asked to 'photograph'.

'Right,' said the Major, smiling, 'we'll have it all again tomorrow when it will be sketched as you describe it.'

He said that Air Force Reconnaissance planes would follow up at certain heights to take pictures; they wanted a 25-50 mile radius. He wanted to know about the attitude of the people, and I told him his friends had been more than kind, but the people in the area were resentful because of all the destruction. The Germans whom I had seen had behaved politely, and people seemed quite free to move about. I had noticed many workmen being escorted to work in the direction of the coast, so assumed that they were on special work. I later discovered they were working on the Atlantic Wall, which was being built along the Normandy coast.

I was not summoned to Storey's Gate after this trip because the PM was away. I returned to the M.E.W., where I found my cousin had filled in well in my absence. She had marked several items which she could not translate, but I was able to do so. All the officers, both British and American, seemed to be working at speed. I am sure this was the American influence. They seemed to be filled with energy - perhaps it was those A1 steaks they were always talking of with nostalgia.

At the end of November, I went to Paris again to see Jacques and try to form some Maquis groups. I was dropped, or rather landed, just before dawn, at a different field. I was able to get to Tours, by a longer route. I felt I was blazing trails for others to follow. When I arrived in Paris I phoned Jacques from the station and he said, 'Come by Metro. I'll meet you.' When I left the Metro there were two Gestapo officers standing at the entrance, and for their benefit Jacques embraced me and made a great fuss over meeting me. As we passed them he touched his hat and they nodded to us. I told Jacques he was asking for trouble, but he just grinned and said, 'It works. They love to be recognised as 'visitors'.

Marie was waiting at the flat, and with her was a friend of

Jacques from the Free Zone. He was introduced as Jules, and Jacques introduced me as 'my friend'. I asked the man how he managed to get into the Occupied Zone – did he have a permit? He said 'I swim well. How did *you* get here?' I replied, 'I pay well.' He laughed and turned to Jacques, saying, 'You are sure she's a woman? She thinks like a man.' He probably believed me no more than I believed him.

We talked over brandies with sugar lumps, dipping them in the brandy and sucking the sugar. I had warned Jacques to tell his friends I was French, and this he did. Jules asked if I could meet him in the Free Zone, near Lyon. Jacques would later tell me when and where. I liked Jules, and he promised me to help in contacts with some men, mostly workers, who were willing to resist but disliked the Gaullists; they simply did not trust them. He asked if I had anything to do with that lot, and I assured him that I worked quite independently. I had a group in the South, but I needed to move in the Midi and Normandy, so wanted contacts there. He seemed quite satisfied with our talks, and left us saying he had other friends to visit.

After he had gone I asked Jacques about forming an escape route from Paris to the Basses- Pyrénées, finishing at Tarbes. He thought it would be very risky. I suggested using the cellars under our flats. He flung up his hands in horror. 'You are quite mad! Have you forgotten Rommel and the German officers next door?'

I said, 'That's just the point. They wouldn't believe anyone could be so brazen. Under their noses – that's the safest place.' Jacques started to laugh, and finally agreed.

He thought schools would be the best places to choose along the route. His contacts in the Midi would help with this. He told me of an escape route over the river Cher. I found out later on that this was the 'Pat O'Leary Line', one of the most successful, run by the French S.O.E. with the help of others in the Resistance. Many farmers helped on this escape route; they had land on either side of the Cher and were allowed to work it. One bee farmer who moved his hives about carried false papers and rounds of ammunition in the hives, and the bees continued to work undisturbed.

When I returned to England the Major approved of our suggestions and said he could help with the schools on the route. The escape route was ready by 1943, but it was rarely used as far as I know.

I was back in Paris in December. Within these few weeks it had changed. The Abwehr (Secret Service) was very active. They had opened a branch in Lyon, but still had their Headquarters in Paris, on the Left Bank. Admiral Canaris was officially in charge, but he did not appear very often. It was Sergeant Bleicher, the hated one, who seemed to have limitless power. He was beginning to show an interest in the Resistance movement which had not emerged before. Up to now he had been after bigger fry - those engaged in espionage.

Jacques asked me if I knew an agent called Shelley. I said I had never heard of him, but actually I knew him quite well. Shelley was a name used by the 'White Rabbit', Wing Commander Yeo-Thomas. He worked mainly with the French S.O.E. The rumour was that Sergant Bleicher was making enquiries about him.

Jacques seemed to know a great deal about Bleicher. It was said he had a mistress who was French, who had an important job with the Anglo-Polish Resistance Group; but she was betraying them to Bleicher. I learnt later in the war that she also betrayed other S.O.E. agents, British and French. The British became aware of this and they invited her to come to England to work for them. This was too good an offer to refuse. Sergeant Bleicher himself urged her to go, and feed back information to him. This she did, but the information was false. Without knowing it, she worked as a double agent, quite unaware that the British were using her. After serving their purpose, she was imprisoned in Holloway, and other closed prisons.

After the war she was returned to Paris for the French to deal with, and was sentenced to death but later reprieved. The last I heard of her, she was living in Paris and was blind, alone and friendless. I hope someone will remember that before meeting Bleicher she did good work for France in the Resistance. We cannot account for the power of love and sex. I should not like to judge her.

Jacques was increasingly worried about some of the Resistance groups in Paris; he felt they were becoming over-confident and careless, talking to one another in cafés and bistros. One could trust no one. Some waiters were in the pay of the Gestapo, and some of his former colleagues in the Communist Party were betraying one another, for gain or for safety. He said he would have a score to settle when war ended, if these traitors were still in Paris.

The Gestapo were more in evidence in Paris at this period. The Military Commander had been replaced by a Nazi Commander, Goetz, who supported the Gestapo and S.S. Pressure was being brought to bear on the Parisians, and one could easily see who was friendly with the Germans and who was not by the harassment that went on. Many streets were now 'out of bounds' to the public; among these was the Avenue Kléber, and I was curious to know why. The French seemed afraid to mention it, and Jacques knew nothing about it.

I was very grateful that I had met Jacques again, for he was so useful and trustworthy. It gave me a sense of security to have a friend in Paris who was in Resistance; the atmosphere in Paris was anything but secure. Yet Jacques never confided the nature of his Resistance work to me, nor did I tell him mine. Our silence was founded on mutual respect and understanding. There could be no success without silence.

By this time I could get in touch with England and did not need to make a rendezvous in advance, which gave me greater freedom. Jacques managed to get me a travel pass through one of his contacts, and Jules met me near Clermont-Ferrand. He explained that the large number of Germans and S.S. troops were there because they planned to take over the Free Zone. They were forming a Militia composed of Frenchmen who were traitors to France.

I met nineteen other Resistance members who were friends of Jules, and Jules made the twentieth. He wanted to join me. My idea was to have four groups with five men in each, but Jules suggested five groups of four men, as each four could work in their own area. Some were on the railways; one was an inspector as was Jules. Five worked in post and telegraph, others in factories, and two had bistros. I told them I was French but worked with some of the British, and I worked alone – I was not a saboteur, I just needed to find out about the conditions and reactions of the French and also, if possible, the movements of the Germans. I did not tell them I went back and forth between France and England. When they realised I was working with the British and they would be helping them, they were delighted. They disliked and distrusted many French Resistance movements. They thought of themselves as Communists, but I did not for one moment look upon them as such. I never really understood the French form of Communism, because so many so-called Communists were Capitalists.

Their only regret was that we were not saboteurs. They were sure they could do a great deal of harm if they were organised.

Later on four of these men were trained in morse and codes and they became my contacts. They were my 'special group'. When I arrived in France they were always there to meet me, and they saved my life on many occasions. I owe them a great deal.

I learnt from their conversations that they knew many of the British and French 'groups' or 'cells', and I was afraid that if they knew so much the Germans might well know also. Too many people knew too much about other people. How wise Churchill was to have a 'loner' moving about - I knew of these groups, but they did not know me.

Jules managed to get me back into the Occupied Zone and I made contact with England. I arrived back safely. It was, I thought, becoming too easy - but I knew that such a thought was dangerous.

When I reported to the Major I told him of the change in Paris and the unhealthy interest Sergeant Bleicher was now taking in Resistance. This seemed to the Major a good sign - the Resistance groups were obviously making an impact.

It was not until early in January 1943 that we went to Storey's Gate. The Prime Minister had been going through a very bad period about this time. The Americans and Russians were pressing for an invasion of Europe in 1943, but he and the General Staff were against it. There was, however, a danger that the Prime Minister in his overworked state might be worn down by pressure from his allies. But, said the Major, he had a great deal of horse sense and Brookie (General Brooke) had great powers of persuasion, and both the Americans and the Russians would no doubt be made to see this combination in action. This proved to be so.

Churchill certainly looked tired when we arrived, but at once became alert, and questioned me eagerly: Had the attitude of the Parisians changed? Were they no longer accepting the Germans? I said there were a great many more Gestapo in Paris and one could sense that people were afraid, but they were now keener to support the Resistance. He was interested to hear about the formation of the Militia - Resistance groups would have to be more careful, especially in the Free Zone. He was very pleased about the new groups I had formed, but when I told him they wanted to do some organised sabotage, and had good opportunities for it, he looked thoughtful. Finally he said, 'I can only say this, Jay Bee - you can take individual calculated risks when the obvious shows itself.'

To myself, I translated this as 'Go ahead!'

We took our leave, and as the Major opened the door a large

black cat walked in. He was about to shoo it out when Churchill intervened with 'Let it stay. I like cats.'

I knew he had a chocolate-coloured poodle he was very fond of, but I was rather surprised to hear he liked cats, and said so.

'I like both dogs and cats,' he said, 'though they're entirely different. Dogs look up to you, cats look down on you. The only animal that treats you as an equal is the pig.'

I wondered what pig had had the temerity to give him stare for stare.

The cat eyed us disapprovingly and proceeded to wash its ears. 'There seem to be several of them about,' said Churchill. 'I don't know who they belong to - no doubt George Rance will know. They have a grand, exciting life, with all the rats. Oh yes, Jay Bee' - I must have glanced round rather apprehensively - 'We have plenty of rats here. Under the Thames, you know.'

We left them communing together.

Back in Sloane Street, the Major gave me my next assignment. He wanted me to go to Paris again. I was to look out for a certain man, a German and a member of Abwehr, who held a very high position but was known to dislike Himmler. There had also been rumours that he did not approve of Hitler's methods. The Major showed me a photograph and said that this man liked 'good living'. He liked a pink champagne each morning at eleven o'clock when possible; and he liked women, especially French and Italian women. All I had to find out was whether he was in Paris. The best places to look for him would be the smarter hotels and cafés. My friends in Paris might be able to help. I would be given one week only to get this information.

It was decided that I should go the same way as on my first trip to France. It would mean a long walk into Tours but I could, if absolutely necessary, contact the new friends I had made through Jules.

8

Prisoner of the Gestapo

My pilot - I had had the same one on each trip - greeted me with
his usual cheery grin as I climbed into the seat beside him. 'I don't
know your name,' he said. 'Mine's Mike.'

'I have no name,' I said. 'You know the rules - no names and no
conversation.'

'Fair enough,' he agreed with irrepressible good humour. 'I'll
call you the Unknown Woman.'

It was a bright, clear night when we left Tempsford. The
country beneath us was like a jig-saw puzzle with pieces of land of
all shapes and sizes fitted neatly together. The rivers, large and
small, glittered in the moonlight. It all looked so pretty and so
peaceful. We flew fairly low over France, and here it was not so
peaceful. The gleaming railway lines, so ruler-straight in contrast
to the rivers, showed movement of trains, obviously goods trains
and troops. There seemed to be many flashes beneath us, but Mike
was unconcerned.

When we reached the rendezvous I was dismayed to see that the
fields had been ploughed. 'You'll have to jump,' said my pilot,
and as we glided down he added, 'I'll see you seven nights from
now, but try and arrange another area for the pick-up. This one
may be dangerous.'

I fell out of the plane four feet from the ground, clung to the
earth, and remained there till the sound of the plane had
disappeared. The Germans ordered the ploughing of the fields to
prevent our planes landing, and of course once on the ground the
Lysander could not have taken off again unaided. I hoped that if
there were any Germans around who had heard the plane, they
would have gone away when it did not land. It was a habit of
theirs to allow a plane to land and then pounce before it could take
off. Mike was a genius with the Lysander. One of his specialities
was to make its engine sound like the chug-chug of a distant motor-
cycle. It would have fooled me if I had not known of the trick.

It was some miles from Tours but a fine early morning. I tidied myself in a small copse - a necessary procedure after falling into a ploughed field. It is surprising how effective a handful of dry grass or leaves can be to do the work of a clothes brush! I met a few people as I walked but they were French workers, and I met no Germans until I reached Tours station. I noticed some Gestapo officers waiting here so I dawdled around looking unconcerned. Experience had taught me that any haste when Germans were about drew attention; I had noticed that people in a hurry were often stopped and, however innocent they might be, were always put through the drill of showing their papers and answering questions.

The train for Paris left without any trouble and I felt quite confident, but also wary. We arrived safely and I phoned Jacques from the Gare d'Austerlitz. He could not meet me, but advised me to travel by Metro and then walk to the flat, which I did without incident. I had always been fond of my flat, but now I looked upon it as a haven. Jacques greeted me with enthusiasm and a brandy for which I was more than ready. I told him that I was in Paris for a week and would like to stay in the flat. Marie, his girl friend, was sleeping there, he said, but could easily move out. I assured him there was no need for this, there was plenty of room for us both and I would like her to stay. She was out at work now, but he expected her back about seven. I asked him if he and Marie could help me to trace a man connected with the Abwehr, one of the former 'Naval Brigade' of Germany, who had the reputation of frequenting fashionable cafés, preferably in the mornings. I told him nothing more about the man, and he did not ask me.

The following morning the three of us strolled about in the fashionable areas like any party of friends enjoying a little leisure and glancing with natural interest at the smartly-dressed customers sipping their coffee or aperitif. We had no success that morning, nor the next. In the afternoon of the second day I told Jacques I would like to visit the Sorbonne area. I wondered how many Germans were in the vicinity; had they taken over any of the buildings? Was the church there being used? Jacques remarked that there were Germans everywhere in Paris and he did not know if the church was being used. He was not interested in churches. The only place of worship he had any interest in was Notre Dame, and not from the point of view of worshipping as he did not believe in God. I felt that he thought of the cathedral as a sanctuary; I had myself on many occasions had this same feeling.

When we reached the Boulevard St Michel I felt at home. The Sorbonne is the centre of the University of Paris. The Church of the Sorbonne is in Jesuit style, built between 1635 and 1642, with a dome instead of a steeple. A feature of this area is the College of France, founded in 1501 as an Institution for Higher Education. Its foundation was a reaction to the Sorbonne, which had a contempt for classical literature. The first subjects taught there were Latin, Greek and Hebrew, but in the nineteenth and twentieth centuries it has been concerned mainly with science. The new buildings which have been added over the years comprise the physical and chemical laboratories; in fact the Pierre and Marie Curie work is continued there.

The Latin Quarter has the kerb-side cafés which are patronised so much by students. It was a great relief to see life continuing normally. I no longer resented this. Our task was to defeat the Germans and to make sure that life - not necessarily life as we had known it - would continue, with the freedom that all human beings could enjoy and not merely endure. This visit to my old haunts brought back memories of the past and filled me with nostalgia.

The following day, very early in the morning, I was able to get in touch with London via Kent, and arranged a rendezvous for a pick-up. Churchill's personal radio code was via Kent and changed every few weeks, only the few who used it knew of its existence. The Bletchley Code Breakers never got on to it. I also phoned one of my Maquis who worked in post and telegraph and arranged for him and two others to be at the rendezvous. I had no doubt that I would be able to keep the date.

On the third day, although the air still had the chill of winter, the weather was fine and bright and it enticed me to venture out alone. As I walked from the Ile St Louis along the familiar pavements Paris, always a beautiful city, looked even more lovely than usual in the late winter sunshine, and I had to keep reminding myself that I was in unfriendly territory on a special mission and had to be constantly on the alert to all that was going on around me. I arrived at a café in the Champs-Elysées and decided that a table out on the pavement would be a good vantage point at which to rest for a while and watch as the people of Paris went about their daily business. If there had not been so many German uniforms about, and Nazi swastika flags so much in evidence, I could almost have imagined that I was back in pre-war days.

I ordered a coffee and casually looked around. There were several uniformed military officers standing about and at a table sat three Gestapo officers. I could tell that they were the dreaded Himmler Gestapo because they all wore the death's head signet ring and had a small dagger attached to the front of a black leather belt. I felt uneasy, and a sudden urge to leave overtook me, but knowing that to act in haste was to draw suspicion on oneself I lingered a while longer over my coffee. Then my attention was caught by two new arrivals, a man in civilian clothes and an attractive young woman. The woman, I was sure, was French, but one glance at her companion showed me that he was the very man I was looking for. I had been shown a photograph, but I had not been told his identity. However, as soon as I saw him in the flesh I knew that my suspicions were confirmed - it was Admiral Canaris, whom I had seen before the war in both Berlin and Munich. I was surprised that he should be Chief of Abwehr when he was at heart a Monarchist and a gentleman and wondered why I had been asked to find out whether he was in Paris. They settled themselves at a table near me, and the man signalled a waiter. They were both quite oblivious of me and of the fact that they were being scrutinised.

This was, indeed, a stroke of luck, and I was thankful that I had stayed. Now my assignment was completed, my coffee was finished and paid for, and there was no reason for me to linger. Yet still I did not leave. I have never been able to define why I stayed at that table. Something more powerful than my own reasoning power seemed to have taken over and I sat on discreetly watching while I pretended to read a French book I had brought with me.

The Gestapo officers looked bored. Presently an old man came along, head down, searching in the gutter. He was obviously hunting for cigarette ends - cigarettes were virtually unobtainable at that time. As he reached the front of the café one of the officers threw down a half-finished cigarette. The old man pounced on it, but before he could straighten up another Gestapo officer stepped forward, pressed his foot on the back of the wretched man's neck and went on pressing until his victim blacked out. I could imagine the cruel power of that jack-booted foot. It was not removed until it had casually crushed out a life. Smiling, the officer turned away and called an elderly waiter to get rid of the body.

I felt physically sick, and although this should have been a good moment to get up and walk away while everyone's attention was elsewhere, I seemed unable to move.

An elderly cripple was approaching, quite unaware of what had just happened, and he too was searching in the gutter. The officers had not tired of their game. One of them flicked a cigarette in the cripple's direction. This time it did not reach the gutter but ricocheted off the table leg and fell near my feet. Of course I ought to have ignored it, but I was so filled with horror and disgust that I forgot all caution and without further thought stood up and crushed the cigarette into powder, grinding it under my heel. When I realised what I had done I could have kicked myself. I was the focus of every eye. It was one of the gravest mistakes I could have made.

As I sat down thoughts raced through my mind. Perhaps the officers would ignore it ... I was conscious of a numbing fear and there was a mist before my eyes. My stomach felt ready to fall out. The mist, as it cleared, became tangible, and as it took shape I saw, standing in front of me, one of the Gestapo officers. The belt and dagger were at my eye level and I was being studied by a pair of steely, pale blue eyes peering out of the mask-like face of a young man trained from childhood to be devoid of emotion. My adrenalin began to flow, and I was quite calm and collected as I smiled at him.

He said in almost perfect French, 'Madame, you do not like Germans.'

I shook my head as if in bewilderment. 'I do not understand. Why should you think that?'

'You do not like Germans,' he repeated coldly. 'You have shown your dislike by interfering. Why did you crush that cigarette?'

I told him I had done it quite automatically when it fell at my feet.

'Why then did you do it in a vicious manner?'

I said I had not realised I had done so, and was sorry, but I had not enjoyed their form of amusement.

'It is not a form of amusement. These people are parasites. They are useless to society and should be removed.'

Before I had time to reply (perhaps fortunately) two other officers came over to me and asked for my work papers. One of them said, 'You are here described as a schoolteacher. I do not think you are a schoolteacher. I would say you are an aristocrat. You have the insolent air of one.'

'Arrest her!' said the other.

I knew my feelings must be hidden at all costs. I must not show fear. I was an idiot. I had ignored the training I had received and the warning, 'Never allow sentiment to overcome your reasoning.' All this had been lost on me; I had failed. I sent up silent prayers for help. A few minutes later a car arrived and I was ordered to get in.

We drove along the Champs-Elysées and then as we were about to turn a corner, I was told to close my eyes. I obeyed, but managed to keep them open just long enough to get a glimpse of the area. We were about to enter the Avenue Kléber. After that I kept my eyes firmly closed knowing that I was being watched by a Gestapo officer on either side of me. Eventually the car stopped and I opened my eyes to find that we were at the back of a large building. I had not known the Avenue Kléber well before the war but I could remember that there was a large art gallery named after the street, and also some other large buildings.

I was escorted into one of these and wondered whether it had been an hotel or a large house. There were many Germans about, some in uniform, some in civilian dress. I also saw one or two women, who I thought looked German; they were certainly not French. I was taken to a room on the first floor in which there were several Gestapo officers – I counted twelve. One of them sat at a desk, apparently in charge. My escort spoke to him in German and was telling him about the cigarette incident. He looked at me intently for a few minutes and then demanded, 'Why do you dislike Germans?'

'I did not say that I disliked Germans,' I replied, 'and I am sorry that I acted as I did, on the spur of the moment. You see, I am a schoolteacher and fond of children, and have always felt that elderly people are rather like children at times, and need protecting.'

The officer was unconvinced. 'I am inclined to believe that you are more of an aristocrat than a schoolteacher. You are certainly very cool and collected. Where do you teach?'

I explained that I was a relief teacher at various schools outside Paris, and was at present between posts. I prayed that this would satisfy him, because I knew that if he continued to question me about education or the authorities he would very soon find out I was carrying false papers. Mercifully he merely nodded, but my immediate relief was soon dispelled when, to my consternation, he told me to strip. With all the self-control I could muster, I forced myself to appear unsurprised at the request and said, 'Do you mean remove my clothes?'

The other officers were all looking towards me. I was determined not to show fear, but my knees were trembling and I felt there was no escape. 'Hurry up!' snapped the man behind the desk, 'Or would you like some help?' There was laughter from the others and I began to remove my clothes - hat, gloves, coat, blouse.

It is said that when you are drowning your past life comes before your eyes. I think this must happen when you are facing any great peril. Many visions of childhood passed before my eyes at this moment, and one particular episode came to me with startling clarity. Five of my brothers and myself had stolen some grapes from my father's greenhouse. One of the under-gardeners was blamed and he was about to be dismissed. We had to do something and I told my brothers I would own up to taking them, as I would not be so severely punished as they would be. Our French governess, who approved of this decision, said to me, 'When you face your father, say to yourself, and look him straight in the eyes when you are saying it, "God bless the Christ in you." Your father will get the message and may not punish you.'

I was seven years old when this happened. I looked at my father and tried to say it silently but could not, and was muttering it between my teeth. 'What are you muttering about, child?' said my father impatiently. 'I have no time to waste. Do go away and play!' I was delighted, and ran off to tell my brothers it had worked - but I completely forgot that I had not owned up to taking the grapes! However, our governess, my dear Colette, told my father about it, and nothing further was said. The gardener was not dismissed.

As I started to undress under those mocking glances all this was going through my head. It can only have been for seconds, but it felt like ages. I was about to undo my skirt and found myself staring at the officer behind the desk and saying silently, 'God bless the Christ in you.' Quite suddenly he said loudly and impatiently, 'This is a waste of time! You may dress.' I did so very quickly. As I picked up my gloves and hat he said 'Leave those! I am inclined to believe you, but you are not going yet.'

He told me that my punishment would be two days' imprisonment, during which I would scrub the main barrack floor and clean the latrines and the officers' boots. This work would be done during the night. I was overwhelmed by a feeling of relief and a desire to drop on my knees and thank God.

I was taken away by a woman who I was sure was not German;

she could have been either Belgian or French, and looked very grim. She took me to an empty room, then pointed to a door which led into a cloakroom. I went in, and she did not follow. I crossed to the window, which overlooked the back of the building. Several huts had been put up there, and I could see a number of soldiers. I noticed that many of them had plain uniforms with no insignia or buttons, and wondered who they could be. They seemed sullen, but were working very hard, carrying things in and out of the huts or sweeping with yard brooms. Two officers stood watching them. These wore the uniform of the S.S.

Was I dreaming? Was all this happening in Paris? I began to think of Jacques and Marie. Supposing the Germans checked my address? My handbag containing my papers was in their possession, and the Gestapo were said to be very thorough.

I left the cloakroom, and rejoined the surly woman. She did not speak, but signed me to wait there with her. It was strange that although I was a prisoner I no longer felt any fear. Two days would soon pass, and all would be well in the end. I have always had a great faith, and it was stronger than ever before. After about half an hour three Gestapo officers arrived carrying books, which they gave me. I opened one and saw that it was in German, as were the others. I thanked the officers, but said I could not understand this language. Was it German? They took the books away and came back with others. These were in French, but about Germany and the New Order and the greatness of Germany, obviously written and printed by the Nazis.

The woman was dismissed and the officers remained in the room and talked among themselves while I pretended to read the French books. I was jubilant that I had fooled them into believing I did not understand German. I could in fact read it and understand it. Now I was going to listen to them.

I gathered that they were expecting a visit from someone important; he was arriving 'the day after tomorrow in the late afternoon'. Later one of them remarked that he hoped he would be transferred to Lyon with the Commander. He had been there before and liked the town - 'He will be taking twenty of us with him.' Another commented, 'It will be different in the Free Zone.' The others laughed. It only appeared to be a Free Zone, said one, the Germans were really in charge; they always had been, without the French knowing it. They found this very amusing. Soon afterwards they went out and I was alone. I saw that the woman had left a glass and some drinking water on a table. I sat down in one of the armchairs which were in the room, closed my eyes, and waited.

Just before midnight two officers arrived with another silent, grim-faced woman. They took me to one of the barracks which was empty and told me I must scrub the floor. They would inspect it at six a.m. The woman showed me where to get water and gave me a bucket and an enormous cloth. I wondered how I was to wring it out. They left me.

9

Unexpected Help

I stood looking at the barrack room floor. There was no furniture, and to my surprise the floor had been swept, but it was still very dirty and its size, like that of the cloth, was intimidating. I wondered how best to tackle it. Many Frenchwomen use their feet when manoeuvring the outsize cloths they use for polishing floors, and I had just decided to try this method with the wet cloth when the door opened and three German soldiers appeared. Each of them carried a pail and broom and one, in addition, carried a chair. He placed it in front of me and in very bad French asked me to sit; they were going to do the cleaning. I could not think why I had been reprieved.

The soldiers worked in almost complete silence, only exchanging a few low-voiced remarks in German, and I saw that they kept glancing nervously towards the door. I realised that it was not a question of reprieve. These men were helping me because they wanted to, and were afraid of being caught at it. They had nearly finished when the soldier who had spoken to me before put down his broom and bucket, came across to me, and told me in his halting French to keep the last stretch of the floor wet. The officers were due to inspect it at six o'clock, and if it was dry they might become suspicious. I said I understood, and thanked them for their help. They smiled weakly and departed as silently as they had come, taking the chair with them.

I still had my wristwatch. At five o'clock, to be on the safe side, I would dampen the part of the floor they had pointed out to me. Meanwhile I sat down on the section of floor which was now quite dry, and thought about the men who had so miraculously come to my aid. They looked unhappy. Who were they? Were they prisoners like myself? They wore plain German uniforms without buttons or insignia like the soldiers I had seen from the cloakroom window labouring under the cold eye of an S.S. officer. They must have been tired, yet they had worked again tonight of their own free will, and had even had the forethought to bring a chair for me. 'It is like a fairytale,' I thought, and could not help smiling as I realised what had been in my mind - an old German fairytale, one of those immortalised by the brothers Grimm.

The boastful miller has told the king that his daughter can spin straw into gold, and the poor girl is locked in a barn and commanded, on pain of death, to spin all the bales of straw before daybreak. As she sits weeping a funny little dwarf appears; he takes her place, the wheel whirrs, and lo! the spools are filled with thread of gold. But the dwarf Rumpelstiltskin laboured for gain, while my Good Fairies had done it out of simple kindness. Yesterday I had seen the dark side of human nature. Tonight I had seen the other side of the coin. I felt a lightening of the heart.

When the officers arrived, punctually at six o'clock, I was on my knees, my skirt was damp and my hands were red from the cold water. I stood up stiffly - the stiffness was not entirely feigned. They looked from me to the floor in evident surprise. 'Very well done,' said one of them to me; then to the others, in German, 'I'd have bet she couldn't do it!'

About five minutes later a woman appeared carrying a tray, and on it was a bowl of soup. I would have given anything at that moment for a drink of cold water, and a cup of tea would have been heaven; however, I drank the soup, as I knew I needed sustenance. I was escorted to another barrack which was smaller and looked very comfortable. The officers' boots were ranged on benches and I was told to clean them. They were made of very good leather, and I could not help thinking of all the Frenchmen who would have been glad of them; many were wearing make-shift footwear, as the Germans had taken most of the leather goods and any left were beyond the means of most French people. The boots were not really dirty and I spat on some, which helped me to get rid of a little of the venom I felt towards their owners.

Next came the latrines. I had mucked out stables in my youth, but these latrines were fifty times more repugnant. I held my breath and managed not to inhale very much.

When I had completed this nauseating task I was taken once more to the room with the adjoining cloakroom. There were some books, four blankets and an armchair. A woman brought me some very watery coffee and a sandwich. She was French, but did not speak to me, and like the others I had met here she was poker-faced. I wondered if she was forced to do this work or if she was a collaborator. I merely thanked her, and made no attempt to get into conversation; she was probably forbidden to speak to prisoners. I was glad I had a drinking vessel and could get water from the cloakroom - it was better than the coffee. The sandwich tasted not unpleasant but was certainly not meat or sausage - a paste of some kind. I amused myself by calling it 'Hitler's Secret Weapon'. I reminded myself that mind was more powerful than matter, settled comfortably in the armchair, and dozed a little.

Several times during the day the door was opened, but I pretended to be asleep and was not disturbed. Eventually I must have fallen into a real sleep, as I woke up to find the lights on and the blinds drawn. No one came with food, and the tray had been taken away, so I drank water from the cloakroom from cupped hands. At midnight the officers arrived, and once more I was left in the large empty barrack. The door had hardly closed behind my warders when my three friends slipped in silently as before, greeted me with their rather sad smiles and set about the floor-cleaning. When they had finished they came over to me and the spokesman said, 'We shall not see you again, madame.'

Somehow, they knew about me and my sentence. I wished I knew more about them. 'Who are you?' I asked. 'Why have you helped me?'

They told me they had tried to desert from the Army. They were not Nazis, they hated these men and the treatment they had received from them. They were waiting to be transferred to Penal Prisons in Germany. I asked if they would be shot. They said no, that would be too easy. They would be tortured or experimented on. They hoped they might be sent to a Suicide Squad; death would then come more quickly.

I found out later that the 'Suicide Squads' were made up of officers and men of the German army who had to be disciplined. They still wore uniform, but they were special cases. They took part in the most dangerous military and naval events. Some were sent to the Russian Front to fight in appalling conditions; some were used to man human torpedoes. If they were deserters or were guilty of a similar serious crime they could be sent to a Penal Prison. These were terrible places, where the sadists in the S.S. gave vent to their 'ideals'. Prisoners had to tackle unexploded bombs or were experimented on by doctors dealing with disease and chemical warfare. Various gases were tried out on them. Few survived the Suicide Squads or the Penal Prisons. It is hard to believe that a cultured race could resort to these methods in the twentieth century.

I felt desperately sorry for these men who had been so kind to me. I said, 'I can only pray for you.'

At six a.m. it was exactly the same procedure as before - the officers, the woman with soup, the boots, the latrines. I thought of Churchill's words: 'The Germans think and work like machines; that is why we shall defeat them. We will dent the machine when and where they least expect it and then we shall destroy it.'

My hat, bag and gloves had been placed on the armchair in the cloakroom suite, and I was able to wash and make up and, above all, to comb my hair. I felt human again and was quickly regaining my self-respect after the humiliations I had suffered. An officer appeared and beckoned me to follow him, and I was taken before the Commandant. He said I had behaved well, and he hoped I realised how kind they had been to me, and that I would tell my friends that the Germans wanted to help the French people and give them the advantages of their New Order. I was now free to leave.

I could not help wondering where the catch was. I was escorted to a car in the grounds, and as I stood waiting for the officers I noticed that one of my three secret helpers - the one who spoke some French - was sweeping the ground near the car. He passed close to me, and without looking at me whispered, 'Leave Paris. This is only the beginning.'

So that was the catch. The Mouse thought it had escaped, but the Cat would be watching at the mouse-hole. The officers joined me and I entered the car. I was told to close my eyes, which I did, as I wanted to avoid further trouble. I was dropped off on the Elysées and received some very black looks from passers-by - they undoubtedly thought I was friendly with the Germans. I wanted to get in touch with Jacques, but dared not make contact with him at the apartments. The Germans might have been there - might even be there now. I hurried to the Gare d'Austerlitz and rang Janine at the cafe, asking her to ring Jacques and tell him to come to the station within the next two hours and to bring some of the money I had left at the apartment. I warned her to be very careful what she said over the phone. She thought it would be safer if she visited Jacques in person, and an hour later he arrived at the station.

I told him all that had happened over the last two days. He had been very worried at my disappearance, but could only wait and hope for some news of me. The Germans had not been to the apartment, which surprised me. Jacques said, 'Perhaps they intend to visit you when you have settled down again.' Yes, the cat and mouse game! I warned him that I had told the Gestapo I was a schoolteacher 'on supply', and if they called he must say I had been sent for to fill a temporary post, but he did not know where. He was not at all alarmed, but I was sure he would be careful. He knew he was dealing with professionals. I told him I was going south and intended to stay for a while in the Lyon area. At this stage he still did not know I went back and forth across the Channel.

After Jacques had left me I had the surprise of my life. Walking slowly towards me was a man who fitted perfectly into the background and into his well-worn, typically bourgeois clothes. He wore a peaked cap that suggested some sort of uniform. The rather stooped shoulders disguised his height, and there was nothing military in his bearing. Was this really the immaculate Major who always seemed to have stepped straight out of Savile Row? I had never imagined him as a good actor.

He looked straight at me and passed without a sign of recognition, so I walked about until my train arrived. It was going to Toulouse via Tours and I would leave it at Tours, still in the Occupied Zone. Passengers crossing into the Free Zone would have to show their papers at the barrier. I hoped I would not be asked for mine, but in fact we all had to show them. Two S.S. officers were examining our tickets as we passed through the barrier, but after seeing my ticket they only glanced at my papers before returning them. I breathed a sigh of relief and entered a carriage closely followed by a rather garrulous woman. A minute later the Major came in and sat down opposite me. I saw now that he wore an armband and had a Railway Inspector's badge on his jacket; the peaked cap was also a mark of his profession.

The woman immediately launched into a flow of conversation: she was fed up with Paris. It had taken her months to get permission to join her son in the Free Zone. She was going to live with his family. He had a very good job with the Germans on the coast. Was I also leaving Paris? I told her I had been back there for a few days' holiday, that I lived in Paris but worked in Normandy, where I was a schoolteacher. She wanted to know where the Major was going. He told her he was on his way home from a visit to Paris. He lived in the West of France and hoped to reach home within three days. He was a Railway Inspector.

I noted that his French accent was exactly right for the part. It had a slight working-class overtone. He turned to me and asked if

I had enjoyed my few days' holiday; he supposed I had looked up old friends. I realised he wanted to know the result of my assignment. I told him I had met some people I had known for many years; but my stay had been especially interesting since I had also met someone I had not known would be in Paris, and I was very glad I had seen him.

'So your visit was worth while?' said the Major.

'Oh yes,' I replied, 'but I did all I wanted to do in Paris, and now I'm quite pleased to be going back to work.'

The Major settled back in his seat with a book, and to my relief the talkative woman, having lost half of her audience, eventually dozed off. I glanced across at the book the Major was reading. It was of course in French - a technical-looking volume on railways!

When the train stopped at Tours I nodded to the woman and the Major and climbed down to the platform (French railway coaches are always perched high above the platform; one needs long legs to negotiate the gap).

I made my way to the rendezvous. Four of my Maquisards were there as arranged. These four, with a fifth who was chosen later, were the only members of the groups who knew that I went in and out of France, but apart from Jules they did not know I was English. This was my Lyon group, but I always thought of them as my 'special group'. Jules was forty years old. He was a Railway Inspector and was also allowed to run a car, so that he was very mobile. Antoine, five years younger, also worked for the railway. François looked about fifty, but I think he was rather less. Pierre was the youngest of the quartet. He was twenty-three, slim, athletic and very good-looking. He and François worked for post and telegraph. They were all quick-witted and utterly reliable. They were workmen employed and trusted by the Germans, helping Resistance only when they were free to do so. This imposed certain limits on their work for Resistance, but it also gave them very valuable advantages, and so long as they kept their spare-time activities secret they could come and go as they pleased.

The pick-up was successful, and I was met as usual at Tempsford by the R.E. major, who escorted me to my flat. The Major was still away, and I would have to wait there till he returned. The R.E. major prescribed bed and a book. I must have looked as tired as I felt. I had been through a very harrowing time. Also I felt a great relief and wanted to meditate, to thank God for the help I had received. It was good to relax and to feel safe.

Two days later the Major arrived, looking every inch a British Major and not in the least like a French Railway Inspector. His first words were, 'Well done, Jay Bee! I am proud of you. Your reactions were worthy of an experienced agent; you played up and gave me the information I needed. Thanks to you and your French friends I have been able to conclude the assignment.' He did not explain the 'conclusion' and I thought it wiser not to ask.

The Major did not yet know of my arrest; when I told him he was shaken and said, 'But you were so cool and collected on the train!' I related my experiences in full. The mystery of the Avenue Kléber was now solved, but I had not been in a position to learn much about it; perhaps others could follow up and find out more about the activities there. I described the conversation I had overheard in the prison about the transfer of Gestapo officers to the Free Zone. The Major thought this would be very bad news for the S.O.E. The situation was dangerous enough there already; he would warn their H.Q. He said, 'I think you must bear a charmed life, Jay Bee.' Charmed or not, I told him, I had learnt my lesson well on this assignment, and would never again allow my sentiments to overrule reason or duty. They did not mix. I would try to become a machine.

He told me he had been several times to the Gare d'Austerlitz, hoping I would turn up before the end of my allotted week. He had been immensely relieved when I appeared. The Prime Minister was away and would not be back in London until next month, and I ought to take a break. 'A real holiday,' he said, 'not in Paris! Do you know Bournemouth?' I said I did, but a week-end would be quite long enough, as I did not want to get too soft. That seemed to amuse him. 'I have no fears on that score, Jay Bee.'

I spent a lovely week-end in Bournemouth. I was quite happy to be alone, but wished I could have been with some of my loved ones. I quickly put that thought out of my mind and began to appreciate the good food. Despite rationing it was delectable - there was an excellent lobster salad for one meal. I supposed the Black Market was thriving in this country as well as elsewhere. The Americans had taken over Southern Command bases, and there were many American Servicemen drinking in this hotel. I must confess they were not the only ones - I had several brandies and thoroughly enjoyed them. 'If ever I take to drink,' I decided, 'my booze will be brandy!'

10

Repression and Resistance

After my Bournemouth week-end I returned to London and slotted smoothly into my job at the M.E.W. as Jo slipped out of it. It was a very odd feeling. So much had happened to me, yet my colleagues were not aware that I had ever been away from my desk.

I had not seen the Prime Minister since before my last trip to France, and it was some time before I was to see him again. In the middle of February 1943 we learnt that a cold which he had contracted in the Middle East had turned to pneumonia and he was seriously ill. I was dismayed, but not surprised. The heavy burdens he had carried during the previous year - decision-making in the face of criticism from Service chiefs on his 'interference'; the stubbornness of some members of parliament; the tug of war between Roosevelt and Stalin - all this had begun to undermine his health. He must not die! The country needed him too badly.

By March he had given yet another proof of his remarkable resilience, and was ready to take up the reins again. It was an anxious time in the Middle East. The combination of Brooke - Alexander - Montgomery was a good one, but Rommel was a hard nut to crack. He had attacked the Americans, who were now lending their weight in the Middle East; his strategy and tactical exploits were beginning to pay off; he turned to attack Monty, who was expecting him. Monty out-foxed Rommel the Fox, who left Africa a very tired man. The command of the Axis Armies now came under General von Arnim, but despite the fierce fighting Monty, with the aid of the Americans and the strategy of the combined forces, gained the final victory, and by May of 1943 it was all over bar the mopping up.

At the end of March the Major and I were escorted to the Prime Minister by George Rance, who was as concerned about the great man as a hen with one fragile but overbold chick. Few people knew of the bond between these two men. George Rance was highly skilled, yet the most unassuming of men. He was in charge of Storey's Gate - providing equipment and was described as the Caretaker. He was much more than that to the Prime Minister who trusted him completely. It was a strange alliance - Rance was a devoted servant of the Civil Service. Churchill was very dependent on him in Storey's Gate.

The Major asked him if he had completely recovered. He said that he had, and was glad Brookie had also recovered from influenza. 'I do not know what we would do if we lost him.'

He had already heard about my adventures from the Major, and congratulated me on the way I had handled them. He hoped I was not being used beyond my endurance. I assured him that I was quite fit, and had learnt a lot from my experiences. I was ready to go back to France any time he wished. He nodded approvingly, and said he would like me to visit the supposed Free Zone again as soon as possible, as there was some information urgently needed. 'This is a vital year,' he said. 'We dare not lose the war. We must defeat the Axis Power wherever it rears its ugly head.'

The Major called at Sloane Street the following morning and gave me details of the information which was urgently needed. The Germans had canalised many of the rivers in France and Belgium. Craft such as assault boats, motor launches carrying twin torpedo tubes, barges carrying ammunition, were passing along the rivers and going through Free and Forbidden Zones. My assignment was to find out as much as possible about their movements. I told him that two of the men in my Lyon group worked on the railways, and two were in post and telegraph. They might know something, or be able to find out. Apart from my own groups, some Maquisards in the Lyon area were with the F.S.O.E. and some were with the Gaullists under the agent known as Max and also Rex. The Major warned me against these other groups; they must not know of my existence. I assured him that my men were to be trusted and preferred to work with me. They did not like the Gaullists.

Three days later I was near Vichy and in touch with my Lyon group. The Germans were much in evidence, but the most frightening development was the formation of the Militia. It was shameful that the Vichy government had allowed this to happen. The scum of France joined the Militia - criminals and sadists, the dregs of humanity, men prepared to sell their own people to the Gestapo, to betray the men and women of the Resistance into torture and death. They were a greater menace than the Germans,

their masters. Many of these monsters were destroyed by the
Maquis after the Liberation, but many others threw off their
uniforms and moved to other districts. I doubt if they have ever
been troubled by a conscience.

The Germans were in full force in the Midi. There were many
S.S. and Gestapo in the Lyon area. The tempo was quickening
dangerously. The Waffen S.S. were moving in, a Force which
included Dutch, Belgians, Poles, Russians, Czechoslovaks,
Austrians and some Egyptians. I did not know any British or
Americans in the S.S., but I heard afterwards that there was a
small group of each. I hoped they were killed in battle.

Fear had invaded the supposed Free Zone. Laval who was back
in the Vichy government had signed papers enabling the
Germans to force young men and women into Labour Camps.
The French had not expected this betrayal. Some hid themselves
away from relatives and friends, but if they were caught their
punishment was severe. My men reported that they had heard the
screams of these men and women.

But if the forces of repression were strongly mobilised, so were
those of Resistance. I knew that the British S.O.E. had many cells
in this area, and also the F.S.O.E., working under the British. In
1943 a new French government was formed on the advice of the
Americans. Its seat was Algiers and its head was General Giraud.
The Americans formed their own Resistance Force; the groups
were under O.S.S. (Office of Strategic Services) led by William
O'Donovan. I do not think they had a great deal of help from the
British or the French Resistance, and I do not think they were
sufficiently trained in the patois of France, but they came in at a
time of great peril to establish liaison with cells, and faced grave
risks. I had the greatest admiration for their courage.

My men told me there was a rumour that Sergeant Hugo
Bleicher of the Abwehr was in the South and actively searching for
the leaders of the Resistance cells. Detector vans were all over the
place and the radio operators of the Resistance had to be
constantly on the move. The Germans hoped to capture the
radios, obtain the codes from the operators by torture and turn
them to their own use. We heard of many arrests at this time.

I was finding it more difficult to move about the supposed Free
Zone than the Occupied Zone, but I was fortunate in having my
groups and other friends on whom I could rely.

The city of Lyon, once the centre of the silk industry in France,
is an industrial city - more inventions came out of Lyon than one

can remember. The Lyonnais people remind me very much of our own industrial townsfolk, especially our Northerners. They all love good food and plenty of it. They are family people and wary of strangers, but once they have accepted you they are friends for life. They are forthright and outspoken in manner, they are staunchly loyal. The men in my Lyon group were such men as this. They had a great respect for me, and the feeling was mutual.

Lyon lies between the Rhône and the Saône, spanned by wide bridges, and they link two distinct parts of France, Rhône and Loire. Amid pine and fir trees the rivers flow in opposite directions. Each region has its own mountains, the Lyonnais and the Drôme, and both produce superb wines. It is a beautiful and an historic area, and famous for its excellent food - superb soups, steaks and chicken cooked in wines as no other French province cooks. I believe that the many Germans who came on leave to Lyon during the war did so because of its reputation for good food and wines.

One of the men in my Lyon group told me he had noticed some ambulances parked in column formation at the side of a wood outside the city. They had been there for over a week and he thought it rather sinister. We decided to find out. One of the group cycled past in daylight looking for cover nearby and reported that there was a fairly deep ditch running alongside the road inside the woods. This seemed an ideal hiding place, so we approached through the wood after dark. We all wore dark clothing and split up the group as an extra safeguard. I walked arm in arm with Antoine, and the others followed at intervals. It was dark among the trees, but as we emerged at the edge of the wood, almost opposite the ambulances, the stars seemed to light up the sky.

There was no sign of life, but we took no chances. One by one and in silence we crept out and concealed ourselves in the ditch. The vehicles looked innocent enough. No aerials showed on them, so I did not think they were detector vans, but I was curious to know what they were doing there. I whispered to the men to wait in the ditch and keep their heads down while I tried the door of the last one - they had wide double doors at the back, like ambulances. They were parked about six yards apart, and the last in line stood about four yards from the ditch. I took off my shoes, stole up behind the van and quietly tried the door handle. It turned, and I very gently opened the door.

A German soldier was sitting at a radio. I closed the door as he turned to look. He had barely had time to see me, but must have seen the door move. I took only two steps, then jumped and landed in the ditch on top of Pierre. Pierre was usually inclined to argue. I don't know whether he kept quiet on this occasion from fright or from lack of breath. We all stayed as still as possible, not daring to move. The door of the ambulance opened and the German soldier came out. He did not look in the direction of the wood, but walked past some of the other vehicles. Presently he returned to his own, climbed in and settled down again. I wondered what he was thinking - perhaps that one of his companions had tried the door for some reason, or that it had not been properly fastened. We waited a while longer before slipping back into the wood unobserved.

When we were well away I told the men what I had discovered - that these were detector vans in disguise. The aerials must be inside. The Germans had made a great study of detecting, and this was evidently one of their latest tricks. The other groups in the area must be warned immediately. As a result of our information one saboteur group took positive action, and some of these phoney ambulances were blown up.

Two days after this episode Pierre, who worked in post and telegraph, told us that he was being sent to the east of Lyon, the other side of the Rhône. This pleased me greatly, because this area was in the Forbidden Zone and only those workmen having special work papers could get in and out without trouble. These papers had the Gestapo stamp - the love birds - on the back, which permitted them to be out after curfew or very late at night. I told him to take particular notice of the river and of any traffic he saw. On his return he said he had observed a great deal of movement on the rivers, and had heard that members of a Lyon Resistance group had been successful in sabotaging some of this traffic on its way to Italy.

He had been in Savoie, and found that the Maquis there badly needed equipment to help them resist. They seemed to be forgotten by other cells. One could understand the difficulty of getting supplies to them, as this was the Forbidden Zone. He thought material could be dropped to them by plane. He said the Germans in the Forbidden Zone seemed so sure of themselves that they were not really aware of the feelings of the people, and would not expect resistance.

I made a mental note of all he told me. I had collected so much information that I was now anxious to get back to England and pass it on. After making my arrangements to leave I told my men I would be leaving the district for a time, but they were to go on with their work and were under no circumstances to work with other groups. Before I was picked up I heard one more frightening piece of news - Eichmann was in the Midi searching out Jews. This spelt danger not only to the Jews, but to the Resistance groups, as Eichmann's men would be working as civilians, and I urged my own men to be more than ever on their guard.

11

Picnic for Spies

I was glad to be back in England and to unload all the facts and the rumours that I had stored in my head; the detector vans; the river traffic; the appeal for help from Savoie; the danger to the Resistance cells, not only from the recent increase in the forces holding them down but also from their own carelessness. Their very enthusiasm made them careless, and they knew far too much about one another. Some of the Vichy Police openly discussed Resistance members and the big ears of the Militia were at every key-hole.

The leader of the Gaullist group, the man known as Max to some and Rex to others, was Jean Moulin. He was doing splendid work, and I heard that he moved about alone. He was loved by his men, and was indeed more popular among them than was General de Gaulle. Had Rex lived, he could in my opinion been President of France, such was his standing with the Resistance. I told the Major I had picked up a message to Max from de Gaulle's H.Q. in Algiers. I thought someone was being very careless - if I could pick it up, then so could the Germans. I thought the different cells had too many 'letter offices' and 'safe houses'. The Germans had eyes like hawks and became suspicious of anyone visiting the same place several times; and like hawks they swooped on their prey.

The Major confirmed the rumour that Eichmann was in the South of France and the Midi, which in turn verified Hitler's order to Himmler: 'Exterminate all European Jews.' This was his 'final solution'.

The Major was delighted that I had collected so much information. I told him that on my next visit I wanted to watch the river traffic myself and he agreed, but said that I must take a few days' complete rest.

I learned that O.S.S. were going to try to get equipment into Savoie. It was later on, in July and August of 1943, that their mission was accomplished. Under the direction of Major General William O'Donovan over three hundred bombers parachuted in equipment and materials. American personnel were also dropped into this forbidden area. If they were caught they could expect nothing but the worst kind of torture. The Americans had only been in the war a short time and sabotage was new to them, but they entered the field with their typical freshness and zest.

I cannot speak of the American contribution to Resistance in France without paying tribute to Virginia Hall a journalist who worked in Paris before the war. Until 1942 she did wonderful work in the Lyon area in connection with escape routes. Many British pilots and French saboteurs were helped by her and she did a lot of resistance work before the Americans came into the war.

When the Americans joined the Allies she was trained as a radio operator and courier with Underground groups. She did splendid work and should have received awards from the Allies, particularly from the British. Nations tend to forget their heroes and heroines.

I was now quite refreshed and arrangements were made for my return to the Free Zone. I used radio only as a last resort, mainly to arrange a pick-up. I was warned to be very careful. Before the war Britain, and I imagine other countries also, had a short wave radio system which enabled our M.I.5 to communicate all over the world. The Major was very emphatic that our code should be used only once. We could change it frequently by adding or subtracting figures or letters and only the receiver and transmitter would know of the change.

At the centre of communications, which was at Bletchley, the back room boys and girls were brilliant; they could break any code. Universities, schools and industry had been combed to produce the brains at Bletchley. I think it is true to say that these brilliant cypher experts were responsible for the defeat of the Germans; perhaps more so than the Service people who carried out the strategy of war. The record of their work was released in 1975. I have heard that some records of the war were deliberately destroyed; others have gone into the archives. The mother of all computers was born at Bletchley and was known as 'THE ORACLE'. It is a great pity that it was destroyed after the war. Our young people today would have loved to see it now that telecommunications play such a large part in industry.

As the Lysander rose up from Tempsford I realised with something of a shock that I was becoming almost blasé about these trips, and that this was to ask for trouble. Since my arrest in Paris I had been determined to harden myself, and in doing so I found that I could talk and think of atrocities as if they were a normal part of life. It was difficult for me to shed a tear, my tear ducts seemed to have dried up. I did not want to lose my sensitivity. There must be some middle way ... to feel, and yet be able to overrule one's feelings ... to function like a machine, but to remain a human being ... was this possible? I prayed for strength to walk this middle way. On the flight into France my thoughts were far away, and I hardly noticed the journey. Unfortunately the landing field had been ploughed up and I had to fall out. This brought me back with a jolt to reality and the mission in hand.

I contacted my men of the Lyon group and found that they had acquired a great deal of information during my absence. The two railway men, Jules and Antoine, had been working in the Forbidden Zone as they had 'love birds' on their papers. This was indeed a stroke of luck. They told me there were rumours that underwater craft had been seen on the river Saône. They were very small and manned by two men only. This sounded rather fantastic, but ought to be followed up. I suggested having a picnic near the river.

We in this country are inclined to picnic within sight and sound of others. The French prefer to be away from other people, isolated in their own tight family circle. The French tourist, for example, would never think of sitting down on a grass verge at the roadside to picnic beside his parked car as the English so often do. He opens a gate and drives right into the middle of a field - an action calculated to rouse the wrath of an English farmer. If there is no gate handy, then all the picnic paraphernalia may be heaved over the wall and followed by the occupants of the car.

Diner, the evening meal, is the most important family event of the day, and *maman* expects all the family to be at home for it, seated round the table to talk and eat in leisurely fashion and compliment her on her cuisine. *Déjeuner* is usually the 'yard of bread and bottle of red' which seems to amuse the English, and when weather and circumstances allow it is more agreeable to eat it in the open. But the most popular type of picnic is the true family one, including all ages and stages; aunts, uncles, cousins, grandparents and small children. Our party, therefore, consisting of one woman and four men of varying ages, picnicking *en famille* in a pleasant spot away from it all, would excite no comment in France.

We decided on a place near some woods overlooking the river, and agreed to find our way there separately and meet up in the woods. Three of the men had cycles and Antoine had a motor cycle. I rode pillion behind him, hugging the square hamper whose sharp edges dug into my tummy. Antoine must also have had a few uncomfortable nudges in the back, but he was very uncomplaining; if it had been Pierre I would have heard about it. It was a pleasant, sunny day, and as I unpacked the hamper we were in holiday mood. Jules had provided the sandwiches. They were about a foot long, of crisp fresh-baked bread with a mixed meat and salad filling. There were two thermos flasks (large miner's size) and two bottles of wine - this was a Black Market area. We laughed and chatted over the feast like any peace-time picnic party, and the war and the Germans seemed far from our minds; yet we never relaxed our observation of the river, which we could see quite well from our vantage point without being seen.

Pierre, who was filled with restless energy, left us finishing off the food and wine and put in a few minutes of his usual target practice, throwing a knife at a tree trunk. He was expert with a knife. When he came back and slid down onto the grass beside us, he began to boast that he could speak English. Before the war he had worked in the stables on Baron Rothschild's estate, and there he had consorted with English stable-lads and jockeys who had come over with some horses. Jules - the only one who knew my true nationality at that time - winked at me and challenged him to say something in English. 'She,' he said, pointing at me with a sandwich, 'being an educated lady, will tell you whether it's right.'

'Of course it's right,' said Pierre indignantly.

'Go on then, say it!' urged the others.

'Shut the bloody door!' said Pierre proudly.

They looked at me questioningly. 'What did he say? Did he say it right?'

'Well,' I said, 'he told you to shut the door, but it would have been better without the "bloody".'

'That's the way they always said it,' Pierre protested.

'I dare say, but it's not necessary. Bloody's a rather unpleasant swear word.'

Pierre looked abashed for a moment, but I suspected the others were memorising it for future use.

'Anyway,' Antoine pointed out, 'there's not much point in being able to say "Shut the door" when we're sitting in a field.'

'I know another one,' offered Pierre. '"Mademoiselle, you want piss-piss?"'

I hooted with laughter. 'Pierre, if you're taking out an English girl friend and say that to her you'll probably get your face slapped!'

He gave me a pained look. 'What do I say to her, then?'

I suggested 'Would you like to go to the Ladies' Room?' or 'Do you want to powder your nose?' Pressed to continue this fascinating lesson, I told them various phrases the girl friend might use, such as 'I must pay a visit' or 'I must spend a penny.'

'Would a man say that?' they wanted to know.

'A man might say, "I'm going to see a man about a dog" or "I must wash my hands".'

When translated and explained, these phrases produced amazement and hilarity. I could not resist telling them one of my favourite stories: A Frenchman was visiting an English family and on his arrival the hostess asked, 'Would you like to wash your hands?' 'Thank you, madame,' he replied, 'I have already washed them against a bush in the garden.'

'Funny people, the English,' said François when the mirth had subsided. 'We Frenchmen, we do not say anything. We just go.'

Typical, I thought. No hypocrisy!

Our banter and gaiety was punctuated by the spotting of river traffic. We counted assault boats, coastal control boats and also motor launches with twin torpedo tubes. Many of these craft would be destroyed by the Underground when they reached a certain point. When I look back I realise what a fine job these saboteurs did. With so little equipment, mainly home-made explosives, their success was phenomenal.

In the afternoon we at last saw what we had been hoping for. Suddenly from the river a craft rose up, and from the distance I saw that it seemed to have a conning tower at each end. A man's head appeared from one of these; after a few minutes the head disappeared and so did the craft. I wondered if there were others with it.

'I think it's going west,' said François.

'The Germans may have thousands of them!' said Pierre. 'They could sink the whole of the Allied Navies.'

'Not in a thousand years!' I countered. 'Don't be such a pessimist.' It was an awesome sight nevertheless. What we must do was to find the pens, if any.

The two of the group who worked for the railways had to

report for duty after lunch, but they rejoined us later. They had seen military movements on the roads; we would have to be careful on our way back. We did have some difficulty, having to dodge German cars and lorries. My men waved to the soldiers as we passed. The Germans loved this, especially the ordinary soldiers. They must have missed their families and friends as did all Service people of all nations.

There were rumours that the Germans were looking for Jean Moulin in this area. Antoine actually knew him, as Jean had been Mayor of Antoine's home town. 'A man who loves France' he described him. Although he was running so many groups Jean seemed to work alone. 'He is like you,' said Antoine. 'No one ever knows where he goes when he leaves them.'

'That is the right way to run a group,' I said. 'If you are caught and questioned you cannot speak about what you do not know. I do not ask you where you go after you leave me and when we are not working together, and I expect the same treatment from you.' They all agreed that this was as it should be.

I moved about a great deal and made many visits to places in the Lyon area. I was not surprised when I recognised several of the Gestapo officers who had been present when I was arrested in Paris. What I had heard in the Avenue Kléber was quite correct - they had been transferred to the Free Zone. I kept on the alert, but had no fear that they would recognise me - my appearance and my papers were quite different here. In Paris and areas south of Paris I was Yvonne Millescamp; I used make-up, my hair was waved and my clothes were fashionable. In the Lyon area and other parts of what was termed the Midi of France the name on my identity card was Joséphine Maisonnave. I wore plain glass spectacles, no make-up, straight hair and less fashionable clothes. I always wore a hat of sorts.

I found out that the Gestapo Chief was a man named Klaus Barbie. He tortured so many men and women that in a short time he became known as 'The Butcher'. This was the same man who had been the Commandant in Paris and had interrogated me in the Avenue Kléber. I was thankful that I had not known his reputation at that time - it would not have been so easy to face him and remain calm. I was indeed fortunate to have been treated so mercifully by the Butcher - but perhaps he had intended to let me settle down and feel safe, and then pounce. It is possible that I owed my escape from further arrest to Barbie's transfer; I had heard from Jacques that the police had not been to the flat. This meant that if necessary I could visit Paris again with little risk.

I had arranged a meeting with Jules and Antoine before I left for home. Friends of Jules had a smallholding near a main road in the vicinity of Châteauroux and I was to make my way there alone. When I arrived at the house in the evening only the wife and an elderly woman, her mother, were there; Jules was expected soon with the woman's husband. The elderly woman excused herself, saying she was going upstairs to rest, and I was left alone with the younger woman, who seemed to be very nervous. I tried to make conversation with her, but she was so tense that I found it very difficult. Jules had told me that his friends had three lovely children, and I thought any woman would be ready to respond to questions about her children. I said I was hoping to see them. She said that they were in bed. I tried again, and was just asking their ages when she suddenly stiffened and turned very pale.

'Can you hear something?' she whispered, as if her breath had stuck in her throat.

'It sounds like a lorry on the road,' I said, and added to reassure her, 'Nothing to worry about. There are lots of troop movements.'

She went to the window. I followed and saw that two army lorries with German soldiers in them were slowing up. The woman was petrified. I don't think I have ever been aware of such fear in a human being. It was like something tangible, like a presence in the room. She seemed unable to speak or to move. I thrust her towards the stairs and told her to go to her children and to keep very quiet. I would deal with the situation as it arose. The lorries stopped and several armed soldiers descended. I sent up a silent prayer.

The German soldiers approached the wall of an outhouse and all of them began to urinate. Then they all returned to their lorries and climbed in. I sat down and laughed helplessly. Never in my wildest imaginings had I dreamed that I should be delighted at the sight of at least twenty men in a row urinating at the same time. I called to the young woman to come down and join me. I hoped that the funny side of the affair would help to drive out her fear, but it was no use. It was too deep.

I persuaded Jules to 'retire' her husband from his work for the Resistance.

On my return to England the Major, who was waiting at my flat, told me we would be going to Storey's Gate that same evening. It was late when we arrived and Churchill was in good form. I confirmed the existence of the underwater craft and he seized on this point immediately. 'Pocket submarines, eh? The pens must be found and destroyed!'

He said that my information had proved very valuable, and I would be going into France more often from now on. He himself would also have to be away more often but the Major would continue to brief me. 'I am sure,' he said solemnly, 'I have never been more sure, that at last we are going to defeat the Nazi war machine.' Then the mischievous glint came into his eyes again. 'I know, of course, that there are still many hurdles ahead - especially for me! They still think I interfere too much. Well - we shall see!'

As we left the Major said, 'A pleasant and safe journey, Prime Minister!' So he was off again on his travels. He seemed indefatigable.

The Major told me to get plenty of sleep and he would see me next day. I inspected my stores and found several jars of peaches in brandy. Wherever they came from, I felt I had earned them.

12

With Orders to Abduct

Late April 1943 the Prime Minister and his staff left to visit the U.S.A. Because of his recent illness he went by sea. The risks were enormous, but the benefit to his health made them worth taking. Meanwhile I was working once more at the M.E.W. The Department was very busy. T.I.S. (Theatre Intelligence Service) was becoming part of S.H.A.E.F. (Supreme Headquarters Allied Expeditionary Force) and the 21st Army Group. Top appointments had not been officially announced, but there was no doubt that the Supreme Commander would be General Eisenhower. I believe that Churchill wanted our General Brooke as Supreme Commander, but I do not think he had any choice in the matter because the Americans were providing so much equipment as well as men and money.

It was not long, however, before I was again replaced at the M.E.W. by my cousin Jo. She still lived in Hampstead, and I was told that she had plenty of social life. Many of her friends were from Yugoslavian royalty, who she helped; she also had a good many Hungarian and Polish friends. Living as I was, so secretly, I could not help being a little envious, but I had not much time for despondency. At the beginning of June I was once more in the so-called Free Zone. It was now fully occupied by the Germans, and the people were suffering all the restrictions which the North had been experiencing for so long, but to an even greater degree. The North had been under good German military command, but now in the Midi and South the Gestapo, S.S., Militia and Abwehr were in control. No mercy could be expected from them.

Eichmann had gathered together hundreds of French Jews. The civic officials in Lyon were forced to help him. They were mere puppets, and had they refused they would undoubtedly have suffered. Life is very sweet to most people, and it was no exception here at this time. The French Jews were placed in one of the prisons awaiting transport to Germany. It was guarded by

Italians. There was a rumour that the Pope had sent in agents to try to get the prisoners into Switzerland. On hearing this the Italian Commander was determined to help, and when the transport arrived the Italian guards refused to hand the French Jews over, and Eichmann had to give in. The French Jews owed their lives to the Italian Commander and guards. Unfortunately the stateless Jews did not fare so well. The authorities were forced to surrender them to Eichmann, who left shortly afterwards.

In the second week of June the Gestapo made a great haul; in a suburb of Lyon they arrested Max (Jean Moulin) and tortured him. Klaus Barbie, the Butcher, was in his element. Max was their biggest catch, a personal triumph for Barbie. It was said that the torture was barbaric, but Jean Moulin gave nothing away. He is still mourned in France by the groups who worked with him. They have tried to get Klaus Barbie back to France to stand trial, but have not been successful; he is said to be in Bolivia. He threatened to betray the names of all the French people who had helped him if he was returned to France, so perhaps it is better that he remains where he is. His revelations would stir up a great deal of scandal and bitterness in France. Many of those who helped the Germans did so through fear, and one can only pity them. The people I despised were the members of the Militia and some of the others who collaborated with the enemy for gain or for the opportunity to exercise their sadism.

General de Gaulle must have felt the loss of Max greatly - Max had kept the General supplied with information. Personally, I thought the lack of information to Algiers might be a good thing. The Gaullist groups were more politically orientated than the others, with the exception of some of the Communists. We were aware of the latter and could deal with them in any emergency, but the General did not always confide in his allies - just the opposite, in fact. One must suppose he had his own reasons for this but his egoism played a large part in his attitudes. He was not an easy man to understand, but there is no doubting his almost fanatical love of France. To him it was a 'Glorious Entity' and must live for ever. I think if I were ever asked, 'What did de Gaulle do for France?' my answer would be 'He made France a respected country.'

I stayed in the Lyon area until the third week in June. At home I found that the general picture of events was looking rather brighter. The first convoy since 1940 had gone through the Mediterranean. On the other hand, the Germans had a tremendous labour force, taken from the various countries they had occupied. They were still building tanks, planes, submarines, etc., and they were getting equipment from factories in France. The Resistance groups were doing splendid work in putting factories out of action, but many of them, both men and women, were captured and paid the price of their patriotism.

My own group played a useful part in sabotage. Those who worked on the railway changed the lading bills on trains, and several goods trains were completely lost, running all over France until they could be unloaded or destroyed by the Resistance.

In July 1943 I went into Normandy. I found that here there were several groups being formed of F.F.I. (Forces Françaises de la'Interieur). My group in the area were very worried about the arrests and torture of the Bretons by the Nazis. Not nearly enough has been said about the courageous Resistance work done by the Bretons. The people were always ready to help our Commandos when they carried out raids, especially those in the schools. Several Resistance groups were run by the headmasters and staffs of schools, especially in the coastal areas.

In Quimper the Grammar School staff did some very fine work. They, joined by many of the Underground, met in the chemistry laboratory of the school. The Germans occupied part of their building, yet these brave men and women carried on. The older boys also helped in the work. They made bombs, including explosive pebbles, and one of their most ingenious products was explosive manure! The outside covering was painted to look like horse manure, and when it was placed in small heaps in the road it needed only vibration to explode it. One of my groups was successful in blowing up lorries and cars used by the Germans with this type of explosive, made in the school laboratory.

When the Germans eventually found out about the activities of this school, they tortured the teachers. The headmaster and his deputy were tortured barbarically until they died, and the Nazis then shot every boy over ten years of age.

I often wonder whether the Gaullists ever thanked or honoured that school. They died because they hated the tyranny of the strong over the weak, and in their love of freedom proved how strong freedom really is. France has reason to be proud of these men and boys and of the other courageous people of Brittany.

On this visit to Normandy I familiarised myself with Caen and Bayeux and the surrounding district, photographing many streets and buildings on my mind. This area was on the Cherbourg Peninsula and it was here that part of the Allied landings would take place. The Germans were being fooled. They thought - and were encouraged through our system of using double agents to think - that invasion would be in the area of the Pas de Calais.

Caen lies about nine miles inland and is known as the City of Spires. Its history is bound up with William the Conqueror and his Queen Mathilde. Several churches were hit during the Liberation, but have since been expertly restored. Bayeux, too, is steeped in history, its main attraction being of course the Bayeux Tapestry, said to have been made by Queen Mathilde in 1077 and depicting the conquest of England by William, her husband. Even during the war both Caen and Bayeux were pleasant places to visit. One had to be careful, but there were few Gestapo or S.S. regiments here. The Army of Occupation seemed to be unconcerned except to 'sit out the war'.

The area of Arromanches was to be used for the artificial harbour (Mulberry) when invasion took place. Arromanches was a pretty little beach town and, it was hoped, ideal for entry. The landing beaches, five in all, were on this coastline. I was glad to see reconnaissance planes in action. Some were coming in at 300 feet to photograph, others at 1000 feet and others again at 1500 feet. They were successful in getting away despite the many German batteries on the Atlantic Wall, which the Germans liked to call the 'Impregnable Wall'.

Much of this area was inevitably destroyed by the Allied landings and the subsequent fighting, but the undefeated spirit of man and nature have between them obliterated many of the scars of war and restored it to its former beauty.

After completing my mission in Normandy I returned to England. I felt that my memory had never been keener or clearer, and I was delighted when the Major told me that my information would be a help towards the Second Front.

My next assignment was a double one, the first in Clermont-Ferrand, the second in the Limoges area. I had a message for Admiral Canaris and had to take back his reply. The message was from Churchill and resulted in the Admiral helping the Allies in every way he could. I now understood why I had been asked to find out if he was in Paris. His French friends were of the 'upper class' of France. Canaris loved Germany and accepted the leadership of the Abwehr because he hoped to destroy Hitler. Unfortunately it was Hitler through Himmler who finally destroyed him, but not before Canaris had given us much help and information which helped us to shorten the war. He did not consider himself a traitor to his own country, but acted as a true German patriot. In his eyes it was Hitler who was the traitor ...

The Admiral was to arrange with one of our country's Service Intelligence Officers to get Hitler out of Germany. I have reason to believe the first attempt failed, but there had been arranged a second attempt to be made after our invasion of Europe. Many Wermacht generals were in this plot, also some of the Waffen S.S. generals who were beginning to doubt Hitler's sanity. They had had experience of being on the Russian Front and found that the Communists of Russia, far from being sub-humans were great fighters and extremely intelligent. They began to doubt Hitler and Himmler.

Rommel headed the anti-Hitler Plot and managed to contact his generals and the Waffen generals who joined them in the plot, (this was in 1944 after our invasion) but unfortunately Rommel was injured on July 17th and therefore unable to progress further with the plot at that time. On 20th July the unity of the progress was destroyed by Colonel Von Staffenberg, chief of staff to Commander in Chief Replacement Army. He carried a bomb in his brief-case and he set it off under Hitler's conference table in Hitler's briefing hut at his H.Q. Staffenberg had left the hut before the bomb went off. Himmler went into a frenzy after this and began arresting and destroying general after general. He began to purge the German Resistance. Many generals and colonels of the Wermacht and Waffen S.S. committed suicide. Those arrested were murdered. History tells us that Rommel later was made to commit suicide. Canaris was also murdered later.

Clermont-Ferrand is the capital of Auvergne and was the home of the rubber industry of France. The many Roman ruins in the area make it a favourite stop for tourists. Unfortunately for its people the Gestapo were there in numbers during the war. It is not far from Vichy, the centre of the puppet government. To call the zone 'free' was a farce. In fact, since 1941 there had been no such thing as a 'Free' Zone. The Germans kept the pretence for the benefit of neutral countries, which still had embassies in Vichy. I did not know Clermont-Ferrand very well before the war, but one of the men in my Midi group knew it well; he had relatives living there. He said, 'Do not trust anyone in Clermont – they are all working with the Germans.' This was undoubtedly an exaggeration, but one had to be cautious. There were many Militia in the vicinity, betraying their own people to the Gestapo. I was glad to be working alone.

After my 'Top Secret' assignment in Clermont was completed I joined my Midi group. I had to get into the Occupied Zone secretly. There are many exits from Clermont-Ferrand and my men knew them all. I knew that the Germans, who might be searching for me after the Clermont episode, would most likely be searching in the supposed Free Zone; in any case my next assignment was in the Occupied Zone. The men said I could only get in by crossing the Cher at a certain point at night. They knew this spot well and used it often, as they had friends in both zones. The side of the river in the Occupied Zone was patrolled by soldiers and dogs, the Free Zone side by Vichy Police.

My men were all expert swimmers. They crossed rivers as easily as crossing a road, even taking bicycles with them under the water. When I told them I could not swim they were astonished. Two things I have tried to do all my life are to swim and to cycle. If I try to swim I just sink; and I wobble and fall off bicycles. There must be something missing in my equilibrium. The men discussed the position and decided that two of them would take me across under water.

I would need dry clothes on the other side to continue my journey, so I had a suitcase deposited at a point near the river and one of the men collected it. It was politely suggested that I strip off most of my clothes, and I found myself quite calmly removing everything except my cami-knickers (a fashionable garment at that time). My outer clothes and the suitcase were packed into a waterproof bag. The men discarded all their clothes and packed them carefully into waterproof sacks. These, together with my clothes and suitcase, were to be taken across by two of the men while the other two swam me over. They held me between them, instructing me to hold my breath and not to move. I warned them that my reaction would probably be to struggle. If I did, they said, they would knock me out! I was glad of my Karate training, as this involved learning to control one's lungs. I told them that I could hold my breath for forty seconds at the most, and they said they would surface twice for me during the crossing. It would be a very brief respite, and they would continue to swim underwater.

We entered the river. I had my eyes closed, exercising 'mind over matter' and willing myself not to struggle. It seemed an age before I was lifted up so that my head was above water. I released my held breath thankfully, gulped in some air and held it. My lungs seemed to have burning irons in them. I was pulled down - surfaced again - the pain was much worse. I vaguely remember being pulled out of the water and carried. We reached cover and I remember being laid down on grass and someone pressing my lungs. I just wanted to die and be rid of the pain.

The next thing I knew was that I was lying on the floor in a room. The pain had gone and four very anxious faces were gazing down at me. I smiled at them and said, 'We made it!' One of the faces disappeared and I saw that its owner was capering round the room, dancing for joy.

The men had brought me to their friends' house - it was a small farm - and I was introduced to two women. They had put me in a warm dressing gown. I had no other clothes on, and I was wrapped in blankets. As soon as they saw that I was conscious they gave me hot soup and brandy. I noticed a clock on the wall. The time was seven-thirty a.m. We had entered the water at midnight! I felt as if I had passed through a whole lifetime.

The men left shortly afterwards, saying they were going to have a look round the area. When they returned they said there were some patrols about but they were not, apparently, interested in anyone in particular. I explained that I would be leaving the next day and going on to Limoges. They stayed only for a meal, and then returned to the Free Zone. I was not sorry that this time they would be swimming without me. It was not an experience I wished to repeat.

I stayed that night with these good friends at the farm, and learned from them that the farmer and the two women were members of a Resistance group. They did not ask me questions and I did not ask them anything. They were very brave people. The farmer had two sons who were also with the group; they were at present in hiding, but were very active. At the end of the war I heard that the two sons had been captured and hung up by their feet so that they choked to death on their own vomit. This was a common practice with the Nazis.

The following morning the farmer gave me a lift to Augusson, a small town, from where I could get in touch with some Portuguese friends of the Major's who I had already arranged to meet. I was successful in this, and went on to Limoges, where I contacted my special Lyon group and discussed my next assignment with them.

Limoges is a very busy town and lies directly on the road and rail route between Paris and the South. It is the home of porcelain and enamels. South of the city a pure white clay can be found which is used in the making of the very delicate Limoges china. This clay has been used in Europe since the eighteenth century, but it was known in China many centuries ago. In Britain a similar clay is mined in Cornwall. It is used medicinally and has many by-products, the chief of which is kaolin. The Germans were making aircraft equipment in the area and there were many troop movements because of the direct routes to Paris.

When I had been briefed by the Major for this assignment it was the first time I had been told to get someone out of France. The man I was to abduct was working with the Germans; if I failed to get him out I was not to worry, but if I could succeed it would greatly assist our war effort. This Frenchman, who had many German friends and a German mistress, had a fear of Communism. No mention was made of a wife or children.

I told the men of my group that if we were successful in getting hold of this man we were to put him on our escape route and others would then take over. On hearing the name of our intended victim, Antoine said he knew his chauffeur. This was a piece of luck for us; it meant that we could find out about the movements of the man and the rest of his household. Antoine discovered that there were five people employed in the house, three women and two men, and all were elderly. There were three more employed outside, one of whom was the chauffeur. The man entertained a great deal so that it was important to know exactly when we could find him alone.

After discreet inquiries Antoine reported that the owner of the house was away for a few days but would be back home the following week-end and would not be entertaining. We planned to carry out the kidnapping around midnight on Friday. My group were all on special work for the Germans and had love birds on their papers, so they could move about freely after curfew. Three of them would be off duty from their work until the Monday following. Jules could not get away, but his place was taken by Georges, who worked on the Marseille docks. After this assignment Georges frequently worked with the Lyon group.

The master suite had been located by Antoine. It was on the first floor, overlooking the grounds, and there was a balcony outside the window. We entered the grounds quite easily through the main gates, which were not locked, following one another at intervals, and found some conveniently placed bushes in which we could remain hidden and yet have a good view of the house. It was all in darkness, but that was not surprising at eleven o'clock at night. We had decided to wait in the grounds for an hour, till we were sure that everyone was in bed and - we hoped - asleep.

This was how I came to be crouching, an hour before midnight, among some ornamental shrubs in the grounds of a large house near Limoges in the autumn of 1943, looking back over my past life and the strange succession of events that had brought me here.

13

Rusty Nails

Just after midnight Antoine suggested that he and Pierre should make the first move; then we - François, Georges and myself - would follow after an interval of fifteen minutes. They slipped stealthily away and disappeared into the shadows of the house. All remained quiet, and at the appointed time François, Georges and I crept forward in the same direction. Suddenly Antoine and Pierre materialised out of the darkness and I sensed that something was wrong. They pushed us back into hiding behind some bushes near the house and Antoine hurriedly explained that they had found the staff entrance door open, and as there was no sign of life they had quietly made their way to the master suite. There they were shocked to find the owner and the German woman, his mistress, both shot dead.

I decided that we should make a search to see if anyone else had been killed, so we cautiously re-entered the house and tiptoed up the staircase, expecting any minute to be confronted by the murderer appearing from some hiding place. We reached the owner's room without incident and found that he was lying on the floor face downwards and that he had been shot in the back of the neck. His mistress was lying on her back nearer the door and had been shot through the heart. I estimated that they had not been long dead. Who had killed them? I wondered if it was an act of vengeance by an underground Resistance cell - possibly a Communist one, since he was known to be anti-Communist - but as it was the usual practice of the S.S. to shoot their victims in the back of the neck it seemed more likely that the Germans had been here. Communist Resistance groups used knives most of the time.

The men had meanwhile scattered to search the house and reported that there was no one else there, dead or alive. The staff had vanished. We did not move the bodies and lost no more time in getting out of the uncannily empty and silent house, leaving everything as we had found it.

This was a turn of events for which we were unprepared, and it was necessary to give careful consideration to our next move. We went into a nearby wood where we were well hidden and sat there for a while pondering the situation. Antoine suggested that we could go to his mother's house, which was quite near. I had not known that she lived here and wondered if it would be quite safe. He assured me that his mother would be in bed and we could leave before she was awake in the morning, so we went to her house and rested there for the remainder of the night. Antoine supplied some wine for the men and made coffee for me, and by eight o'clock we were back in the wood.

Antoine and Pierre went into the town to find out if there was any news of the deaths. A friend of theirs owned an *estaminet* and was usually up to date with everything that went on in the neighbourhood, but he had heard nothing. It was now Saturday, and although the two men moved freely about the town they learned nothing of interest and everything seemed to be normal.

We decided to visit some friends, Jeanette and Robert, who owned a small farm a few miles away. They were members of a Resistance group and Antoine had worked with them on occasion. Their group was one of those that Jules had helped me to form in the area. They did not know of my activities and did not ask questions. We were always pleased to visit them because we were made to feel welcome and Jeanette was a wonderful cook. She baked excellent bread and made a soup which we christened 'garbage de Lyon' - everything edible in sight went into the pot, with mysteriously tasty results.

We stayed on the farm until evening, and then went back to Limoges to see what was happening. Talking over coffee and brandy at the *estaminet*, we heard that there was no excitement. There were many Germans about, but still nothing was being said about the deaths. My thoughts were still confused. Perhaps the man was a double agent working for the Allies and the Germans had found out. Perhaps his mistress had killed him - but in that case who had killed her? The Major had told me not to worry if I failed to get him out. Had he been in danger, and had I been sent in to help him? Where were the staff? My mind was going round in circles.

Antoine suggested he should go to the house again on the pretext of visiting his friend the chauffeur, but I thought this was a very unwise move and dissuaded him. As the men were due to return to work on Monday, I told them to leave me and return to their homes. I said I would get a room at an hotel. In the end they decided to stay in Limoges until the following day, Sunday, at a safe house they had often used. I asked for the address, and Pierre replied, 'You have never before asked where we go after leaving you - why now?' I explained that it was a precaution only. The murders remained a mystery and I was uneasy, and might have to get in touch with them in a hurry. They gave me the address, which I memorised. It was the address of a doctor's house and surgery.

There was a small hotel quite near, where I might be able to get a room, and the men went with me to make sure I was successful before leaving me. It was about nine forty-five; I had just beaten the curfew. The man at the reception desk gave me a key to a room on the first floor. He did not ask to see my papers, and told me I could sign the register later. I thought he seemed nervous. I saw some members of the Militia in the salon with women. Perhaps their presence accounted for his nervousness.

I went upstairs and walked along the corridor to my room, and on the way I noticed a room with its door open and some Militia playing cards in it. I went past quietly and they did not look up. There was a bathroom next to my bedroom and I had a very refreshing bath and went to bed. It was nearly eleven-thirty. I lay comfortably in the dark puzzling over recent events and must have fallen asleep, because suddenly I was sitting up in bed wide awake and a voice in my head was saying, 'Get out of the hotel. There is danger here ... danger ...' The words kept repeating themselves insistently. I got out of bed and dressed quickly. The time by my watch was three-thirty. I wondered if there would be a night porter on duty and if the Militia were still in the hotel. I put my shoes with my other belongings into my overnight case and wore my slippers. I opened the door very quietly and looked along the corridor. It was empty, so I walked slowly along, making no sound in my soft slippers. There was a murmur of voices coming from the room where I had seen the Militia, so the door must still be open. I crept past very cautiously; they were still there, engrossed in their cards. I got past without being seen, but my heart was pounding.

There was nobody about on the ground floor and only a dim light. I reached the entrance door and found it locked, but the key was in the lock so I turned it and went out into the street, locked the door from the outside, and pushed the key through the letter box. I did this quite automatically. It was only after I was standing in the street that I realised I was out after curfew and a patrol might come along at any moment, or some Vichy Police or Militia. I was still wearing my slippers. I felt a bit foolish to have landed myself in this situation because of instinct, but I knew that I had to obey it. What was I doing to do now? Then I thought of the address of the doctor's house where my men had gone. It was not far away. I hopped in and out of doorways, waiting and listening at intervals, and in this way reached the house without incident.

I rang the bell several times before the door was opened and a very irate man asked me what I wanted at this time of night. I slipped past him and entered uninvited, and to my relief he closed the door after me. I explained that four of my friends had told me they were spending the night here. 'Who are you?' he demanded suspiciously. I told him that I sometimes worked with these friends. 'Are you the woman compatriot they were with yesterday?' he asked then, and when I said I was he agreed that they were there. I did not know how far he was to be trusted, and hoped they had said nothing to him about the murders.

'I understood,' he said, 'that you had a room at an hotel.'

I told him that I had had a sudden feeling of danger, so had left.

'I suppose you lost your nerve,' he said.

I assured him I had done nothing of the sort, I had simply followed my hunch, a thing I had always found it wise to do, and asked if I could stay in the house till morning.

'I can't offer you a bed,' he said doubtfully, 'unless I wake the men. They are sharing two rooms. I dare say they would give one up to you.'

I told him he must certainly not rouse them. I noticed a large chair, rather like a dentist's, and asked if I could sleep there. He gave me a nod and left me. The chair was comfortable and I soon dozed off and did not wake again until Antoine brought me a welcome cup of coffee at eight-thirty. I was telling him why I had left the hotel when we were joined by Pierre, who was always rather scornful of my faith and commented, 'I suppose your God warned you? *I*'d call it sixth sense - or perhaps just nonsense.'

Antoine was uneasy. He said there were a great many Militia about. At this point the doctor came in and asked me the exact time I had left the hotel, and when I told him about three-thirty he said, 'You were lucky. The hotel was searched by the Gestapo at four-thirty. I suppose the Militia knew they were coming and were waiting for them.' Pierre gave me an odd look.

I felt safe as far as the hotel was concerned for I had not signed the register, and the receptionist would certainly not report my presence as it would mean trouble for him. He must have been very glad that I had disappeared without a trace. The doctor told us we would have to wait in the house until the excitement had died down - the Gestapo were searching a number of hotels. We had more coffee and some rolls while the doctor went away to make enquiries. Presently he came back and said the Germans were now searching houses, and he was certain they would search his. He suggested that we hide in the cellar, which was a large one, a former wine cellar. We inspected it and found that the lock to the door was broken. The doctor said we had better nail it up. Antoine reminded him that he would have to nail it up himself, as the nails must be on the outside of the door. 'And you must use old nails,' I heard him say. 'Rusty ones if possible.'

The doctor gave us some blankets, some wine and water; there was no time to get food. He told Pierre to take a pail down. In fact two were taken down, for us to use if we had to remain there long. I took my case with me - nothing was left that could betray our presence in the house - and was glad to have my sponge bag and some eau-de-Cologne. The cellar had a strong smell of dampness and stale wine. There was a window at one end, which had been covered. Pierre broke a pane of glass to let in some air and then replaced the covering. Part of the cellar was above ground level.

We heard the doctor hammering, and Pierre the pessimist said it felt like being nailed into a coffin. Supposing the doctor was arrested? We would be left here to die. I said if necessary we could break the door down. I did not know how we could do this as there was nothing in the cellar but a few empty cobwebbed bottles, but Antoine said cheerfully that he had brought an axe down with him. We had not thought of it, or noticed until now. Dear Antoine! He was always the sensible one.

I told the men that if the Germans tried the cellar door they were to try to relax, not to hold their breath as this would make them start coughing. I showed them how to breathe under the effects of fear and fatigue. We hoped that we would be in the cellar for only a short time, but the long day wore on and evening came. A little light had filtered in through the covered window, but now it was almost completely dark. The men had a torch, but we did not dare to use it. Then we heard voices. They grew louder, and we heard footsteps. We froze. I felt rather than saw some movement beside me; Antoine had picked up the axe.

A voice demanded, 'What's in that cellar?'

'Nothing,' said the doctor. 'It hasn't been used for a long time.'

Someone was pushing the door. Then another voice said in German, 'It's a waste of time. Can't you see the nails are rusted? It's been nailed up for years!'

We waited. A moment later the steps and voices receded and we breathed normally again.

I heard Pierre swallow hard. Then he said defiantly, 'I suppose you're going to say your God saved us.'

'It was the nails that saved us,' said Antoine quietly. 'How fortunate that the doctor used rusty ones.'

Antoine never took credit to himself. He was a very fine Frenchman, brave, intelligent and modest. I always feel privileged to have known him.

We waited for the doctor to release us, but nothing happened. Now that the tension had been broken the waiting seemed worse, because we did not know the reason for it. Pierre said the doctor must have been arrested. I thought this was unlikely, since we had not been found in his house, and suggested that he was just being careful, as the Germans might not have left the neighbourhood. They might be searching other houses nearby. Midnight came, and although I was worried I said we should try to get some sleep. I did not feel hungry, and wondered whether the men did. I drank some water, and the men drank some wine, then I wrapped myself in a blanket and with my case as a pillow settled down and hoped to sleep. My eyes were burning. I wanted to weep to relieve them, but could not. I thought perhaps it was better so. My tears might be misunderstood and I was anxious to keep up morale, especially as Pierre was so despondent.

I fell asleep at last and woke to find that my head was resting on Pierre's leg. My face felt very stiff. I touched it with my hand, and found that it was wet. Pierre told me that I had been weeping for hours in my sleep, and he had been wiping my tears away. He did not sound at all cynical.

My eyes felt as though heavy stones had been lifted from them. I tried to explain to Pierre how for some time I had been unable to weep, and how much I had prayed to be able to.

'At least we have all managed to get some sleep,' said Antoine. 'I hope the doctor hurries up. It's Monday, and we all have to report for work.'

'We shall be released before nine,' I said. 'I'm convinced of this.'

'If you say so', said Antoine.

Then surprisingly Georges, who hardly ever opened his mouth - when he did he spoke with a strong Marseille accent - remarked, 'I do not believe in your God, but I have been thinking, and I believe there is a Universal Force - there is *something*!'

Antoine said, 'I think the same.' Pierre and François merely grunted.

It was nearly a quarter to nine when we heard footsteps approaching the cellar - only *one* set of footsteps this time! Then came the welcome sound of nails being pulled out of the door. The doctor opened it and explained that he had not dared to let us out earlier, as the Germans and Militia had still been hanging about, but there was no sign of them now. He saw that both the pails were empty and asked how we had managed. Antoine said they had not wanted any unpleasant smells, and I knew that the men had restrained themselves out of consideration for me. There was a rush to the toilet now and the doctor showed me to a bathroom. There was plenty of hot water, and I soon felt that I was back in circulation after being in a sort of limbo.

I examined the hearts and lungs of the men and found that they were in fine fettle, and so was I. When you have had Death as a companion it is a wonderful feeling to have escaped from his clutches. We thanked the doctor for his timely help and at ten-thirty we made our way separately to Jeanette's, where we had wine, soup and some of her lovely home-made bread. We still did not know the answer to the murders. With the exception of Pierre the men had to go to work early in the afternoon, and when we said goodbye I told them I would be away for some time, but would be in touch. Jeanette and her husband went on with their work about the farm, and Pierre and I were left alone.

To my surprise I found that Pierre wanted to talk about our recent experiences. He asked me about God and Georges' 'Universal Force.' He said he could not believe in a God who allowed all this killing and suffering. 'God does not allow it,' I said, 'it is man who allows it. Human beings create evil. God created man, but He did not expect that as man evolved he would go on behaving as he does. Nearly two thousand years ago God sent us His son in the image of man to show us how love and compassion could overcome evil. Some have learnt this lesson; others are slower, but in time we shall all learn it, and then we shall know why we were created, and the true purpose of life. Some day there will be *World Government* here on earth, not

World Control, where there will be no barrier of creed, language or colour. It may take many thousands of years yet before we reach this stage of our evolution, but it will come.'

'Unless,' said Pierre, 'some idiot destroys the world first.'

'Some part of the world may be destroyed,' I said, 'but there will always be men who have the courage and faith to build it up again. Life is not haphazard, Pierre. There is a plan, I do assure you.'

'I wish I could believe that,' said Pierre.

'Don't worry,' I consoled him, 'you are practising much more Christianity in your way of life than many people who profess to believe.' I was reminded of two verses of a sonnet by Gérard de Nerval which has always appealed to me, and I quoted:

> 'Homme, libre penseur, te crois-tu seul pensant
> Dans ce monde où la vie éclate en toutes choses?
> Des forces que tu tiens ta liberté dispose
> Mais de tous tes conseils l'univers est absent.
>
> 'Respecte dans la bête un esprit agissant,
> Chaque fleur est une âme à la nature éclose,
> Un mystère d'amour dans le métal repose
> Tout est sentient et tout sur ton être est puissant.'

This is a literal translation of the verses:

> 'Man, free thinker, do you believe that you alone
> can reason in this world where life blazes everywhere?
> Your liberty controls the forces in your grasp,
> but your laws have no power over the universe.
>
> 'Respect the spirit that works in animals,
> every flower is a soul open to the forces of nature,
> a mystery of love lies in the heart of metals.
> All things have feeling and everything is a force
> that moulds your being.'

Pierre was quite impressed and said he wished we had more time to discuss these things. He would like to learn more, but our time seemed to be always taken up with our missions. I answered that this was our work, we had to make sacrifices so that others could be free. By working in the cause of freedom against tyranny we were, in a sense, practising Christ's teachings. Christ preached love and compassion; unfortunately we had to do things which seemed to be inspired more by hate than by love, but I was sure that we would be judged by our intent and motive rather than our actions.

Pierre said he had learnt a great deal from the ordeal of the last few days. He was due on duty at 9 p.m. As he left he took my hand and kissed it. This was something indeed coming from Pierre! I was deeply moved.

Some thirty hours later I was back in England. We never discovered who had committed the murders, or why.

14

Operation Stink

'Perhaps it's for the best that he's dead.'

The whole affair of the kidnap attempt and the two murders had been a mystery to me, and the Major's comment did not enlighten me. In spite of his words he was clearly disturbed by the news. I wanted to ask if the man had been one of ours, but did not dare. When I told him the full story of our ordeals he was astounded, and could only say, 'Jay Bee, you are protected in some way.'

He was delighted about the success of the first, the 'secret' assignment involving Admiral Canaris and then said, 'Now forget it.' I told him I had made contact with his Portuguese friends, and how efficient they were. It was most useful to us to have friends from neutral countries who lived in France. They were not harassed by the Germans, and could often provide us with information and help us in various ways. Of course there were also neutrals who helped the Germans. It worked both ways. These Portuguese friends had heard a rumour from Madrid that America's Alan Dulles had met one of the German princes who lived there, and that they were discussing a 'Conditional Surrender' of Germany. Quite a number of Germans were trying, via Switzerland, to negotiate, but Churchill was adamant. The Germans must be defeated. Surrender must be unconditional.

When I passed on the rumour the Major wondered whether the President of the U.S.A. was pulling a fast one, but he felt sure that Anthony Eden, the Secretary of State for Foreign Affairs, would deal with the situation. Churchill had great faith in Eden and considered him the most honest of all politicians. He had in fact said repeatedly, 'If I should die or be killed, Eden must be the next Prime Minister.'

'Do you like Anthony Eden yourself, Major?' I asked.

'Very much,' he replied, 'but he is so honest and sincere that this war is very painful to him - there is so much intrigue.'

We visited Storey's Gate the next evening. Normally George Rance met us, but he was not about and there was a lot of activity in the cellars. Someone stopped the Major and he told me to go on by myself. I had only taken a few steps when I ran into Ernest Bevin. He stood in front of me, tapped me on the shoulder and said, 'Well done, lass!' I said, 'What do you mean?' He smiled and said he knew all about the Secret Circle. I told him I had no idea what he was talking about, and was very relieved when the Major joined us and hailed him with, 'How are you, Ernie?'

Bevin said he had just been congratulating me. The Major put his finger to his lips. I felt thoroughly embarrassed, but Bevin turned back to me and said, 'I don't agree with that description of you.'

'Shut up, Ernie!' said the Major. Then he laughed and said, 'Come along, Jay Bee.'

Ernest Bevin grinned broadly as we left him but I was not amused, and was determined to ask the Major what it was all about when the opportunity arose.

The Prime Minister came out of the Map Room and greeted us, but he looked very grave and was wrapped up in his own thoughts. He had travelled thousands of miles since we last saw him, and pressure was being put on him by both Stalin and Roosevelt to invade Europe. He seemed to stand alone in insisting that we were not yet ready. We must not invade until we were so prepared that we could be sure of success.

He turned to me and said that I had justified the confidence placed in me - always pleasant words to hear. 'I shall be away for several weeks,' he told us. 'I'll see you again in December.' We realised that he had a great deal on his mind and wished to be alone. As we walked back to my flat I felt depressed at seeing him so burdened, and the Major, too, was quiet and did not come in. When he arrived next morning, however, he said to my surprise that we were going back to Storey's Gate that same evening. Something very urgent had come up. He had a luncheon engagement, but would come back about six o'clock as there were matters he wanted to discuss with me.

I did not intend to let him get away before I found out the meaning of what Ernest Bevin had said. I thought that for once the Major looked rather caught out. Pinned down, he said that when the Canaris mission was being discussed it was considered an impossible one. No man could get away with it. Someone had then suggested a woman might succeed, but this idea was also scorned. It would take more than sex to bring it off. Churchill had nodded, and then said, 'But supposing we had a woman who was ninety-five per cent brain and five per cent sex?'

'A robot!' said someone else. 'Why, have you got one up your sleeve?'

'And that was supposed to be a description of me?' I inquired.

'It was meant as a compliment, Jay Bee!'

'I'm glad to hear it,' I said, 'but do you think it's a true description? Only five per cent sex?'

He gave me a very human grin. 'That's an unfair question, Jay Bee! Don't tempt me!'

'Now at least I know *you*'re not a robot!' I retorted. 'I've often wanted to pinch you to find out.'

'I'd better get out of here quickly!' he said, the grin lingering as he left for his luncheon date.

He arrived back just before six and we got down to serious business. He asked me if I had noticed any unusual activity in the area of Bayeux and Caen, and had any of my group seen anything of the Atlantic Wall. I said my men had remarked that there were more strangers about. They thought they were from Paris and working with the Gaullists. There were rumours that the agent Shelley had been in the area and was working with the newly-formed Interior Army, the F.F.I. There was a very good Resistance force in the Bordeaux district and some of the men attached to the S.O.E. there did sabotage in Normandy. They were working under a Frenchman known as 'Scientist' in S.O.E.

The Germans were boasting that the Wall they had built all round the Normandy coast was impregnable. It was difficult for French workmen to get near; even though they had the Gestapo stamp they were always escorted to work by Germans. It was rumoured that Resistance groups had tried to explode the Wall and the submarine pens, but they needed heavier explosives than they could get hold of. They cracked part of the Wall but it was soon repaired and security was even more drastic afterwards. Two of my men who worked for post and telegraph had heard rumours of secret cables being laid in Normandy and in the Pas de Calais area. It seemed a well-founded rumour that the Allies would try to invade there – both German Command and the French people believed this.

My men were sure that the new Resistance groups in the area were talking too much, and as much of the Coastal Zone was 'forbidden' they were making it very risky for other groups and would eventually attract the attention of the Gestapo to this part of Normandy, where up to now Resistance had hardly been noticed. If it was known that Shelley had been seen there it would be enough to bring the Gestapo, who at that time were looking for him in Paris.

When 10 Downing Street was bombed a flat had been made for the Prime Minister at Storey's Gate - a very secure one. It was here that he received the Major and myself that evening. He said that we needed information on the cement that the Germans were using for the Atlantic Wall and that a man had been traced who was an expert on cements. It was believed by his firm, one of the largest in the world, that he was dead, but there was some evidence that he was alive and working for the Germans. The man was English, but he had been naturalised French after his marriage to a Parisian. His parents had also lived in France. His father had died, but his mother lived in Paris.

Churchill asked if I thought my men could trace this man. I reminded him that none of my men were in the Paris Zone, only Jacques, the concierge. I thought, however, that if we contacted Jules, near Lyon, he could get in touch with Jacques; the latter had friends in most of the government offices and railway booking offices. I suggested that the Major's Portuguese friends might be able to help. I had told them about Jules and the trust I placed in him. This was agreed, and we were asked to lose no time, as the matter was urgent.

It was already early morning when we got back to my flat. I made coffee and sandwiches and we discussed the next moves. The Major said he would contact 'our parties' that evening. Within four days we had the information we wanted. Jacques had traced the man, but not his wife or mother. He was very much alive and living in Lyon. According to the report he had been transferred there and was working for the Germans. We were given the name of the Lyon hotel where he was living, and when I heard it I became very interested.

One evening when Antoine, Jules, Pierre and I were passing this hotel we had heard women's screams coming from it. Two Vichy policemen were standing near, and we had suggested they should go into the hotel and investigate, but they told us to move on, saying, 'It is better not to ask questions here. The hotel often has brothel girls visiting clients; it must be one of them screaming.' We walked on, but Pierre was far from satisfied and said he was going to try to get a room there the following

Saturday. I suggested the screams might be from women and girls who had tried to escape the labour round-up and been caught. Antoine said he had noticed Gestapo officers using the hotel.

Pierre did try to get a room there but was told it was fully booked and it was not likely there would be any vacancies for months ahead. I did not believe the story of brothel girls visiting there. The Gestapo had one particular brothel on the outskirts of Lyon exclusively for their own use. I knew Madame, the Procuress. She was trusted by the Germans but she was a good friend to my group and to me; I had treated her when she was ill before the war. Her way of life might not be approved of by many people, but brothels in France were licensed by the government. It was a profession. I liked and respected Madame very much and I knew and helped many of her girls. The Germans allowed her to have a car and a small van. She purchased food on the Black Market for them, charged them more than she paid for it, and gave the profits to the Resistance. Her van was never searched and she often had an escapee in it, transporting him to a safe house or on to an escape route.

She also occasionally sheltered Allied airmen in the house while they were waiting to escape. I was indirectly involved in one such episode. A young British airman was smuggled into the brothel and had to remain there for a whole month because he had such large feet. He was wearing flying boots, and it was not safe to move him without civilian footwear. The neighbourhood was scoured for boots or shoes, but none could be found to fit him. In the end Madame approached me, I got a message back to England, and an outsize pair of boots was parachuted in – just in time. The young man was quite happy where he was and in no hurry to leave, but his departure was precipitated. A German officer, a habitué, walked straight in and up the stairs unannounced and went into the room of his favourite girl; unfortunately the airman was there chatting to her. He left hurriedly. The girl told the officer that her sixteen-year-old brother was visiting her. As the airman – twenty years old but very young-looking – could speak no French, it was fortunate that the officer accepted the story; but the fugitive had to be got out of the house without delay.

I had not had occasion to mention the hotel and our suspicions of it to the Major before, and he was very interested in what I told him and wondered what the English concrete expert was doing there. He would report it all and then a plan of action could be decided on.

We were back at Storey's Gate the following day. It was early evening, much earlier than usual for our visits. The Prime Minister having already been put in the picture asked, 'Jay Bee, do you think you could get into the hotel?' I told him I was quite sure it was impossible; obviously the hotel was occupied by the Gestapo; we had watched them going in and out. The Butcher visited it often, and even Himmler had been seen there with his bodyguard.

'Who is the Butcher?' Churchill asked. I told him it was the name given to Klaus Barbie, the man in charge of the Gestapo in Lyon - the same man who had sentenced me in Paris. I had been lucky there, I had been able to bluff him, but his reputation in Lyon was evil. He was a sadist who particularly enjoyed torturing women and did so in the most terrible way. The Major said it seemed to be a very tricky and dangerous operation, but it was essential to get someone in with a legitimate reason to make sure the man was there.

'I wonder,' said Churchill thoughtfully, 'I wonder if the Prof could help.'

The 'Prof' was Professor Lindemann, the Scientific Adviser to the Prime Minister. He was duly contacted and came up with an idea. He decided that the best way to attack the operation was to drop a very pungent-smelling chemical in capsule form into the drains outside the hotel. The unpleasant smell would then penetrate the hotel by way of the drains. This should lead to workmen being called in to investigate the smell, in which event four of my men, masquerading as plumbers, could go inside and look around.

There was a decidedly mischievous twinkle in Churchill's eyes, which often happened when something amused him; he reminded me of an imp enjoying the contemplation of upsetting things. 'Splendid!' he said. 'That should get them yelling for help. We shall need a full description of the interior of the hotel; we shall have to know whether our man is living with the Nazis; where his rooms are; and above all a way of escape for Jay Bee if she succeeds in getting into the place.'

The Major looked at me and nodded. 'Once we have the report, Prime Minister, I'll work out a plan with Jay Bee. If anyone can carry out this assignment, I feel she'll do it.'

'I agree with you,' said Churchill. 'What an adventure!' I could see that he was still relishing the thought of that horrible smell, and wishing he could have been one of the 'plumbers'.

Three days later the capsules were ready. I took them into France where I had to choose men from my Lyon group who were not on special work. Some of Jules' men did not have regular jobs; they acted as saboteurs for him. They were men of middle age or older who could adapt themselves to any circumstances. It was they who changed the lading bills on trains and sent them travelling all over France, and they were equally successful on the food trains going to Germany. They poured an acid onto good food so that it would be rotten by the time it arrived at its destination.

When I briefed these men they, like Churchill, showed a boyish enthusiasm at the idea of creating a stink. They were given the capsules to drop into the drains and a further number which, if they were able to get in as workmen, they could drop into toilets and other places to increase the smells. Luck was with them. Workmen were sent for to investigate the trouble, and my men took the place of four of them. Not only was the hotel affected by the smells, but also several adjoining buildings.

After I had given the men the capsules I went into a village near Lyon and waited for the report to come in from Jules. They had been successful. The Englishman was in the hotel where he mixed with the Gestapo and had his meals with them. They noted that his bedroom was on the second floor overlooking the street. There were small balconies in front of the windows making it possible to get in from the outside if necessary. The men thought that there must be a way in and out which was not visible and they wondered if it could be via the cellars. These were nailed or screwed up, but the screws were quite new so that it looked as though this had been done quite recently. The back of the hotel overlooked a cul-de-sac and most of the reception area faced this.

To the right of the reception desk there was a corridor, at the end of which was a Ladies' Room. They found the door to this locked, and when they asked to inspect it they were told that it was no longer a toilet and powder room, but was used as a store room. They did not believe this, as one of the men was sure he had heard a toilet being flushed. They could not insist on inspecting it, as this might have aroused suspicion.

The men inspected the cul-de-sac to find out the number of windows on the ground floor. They noticed that there were two small windows in what was obviously the Ladies' Room, or 'store room' as they had been told. The windows were of frosted glass so that one could not see in or out. There was of course no way of opening them from the outside, and they could not see how they were fastened on the inside. I was sure that the 'store room' tale was a fabrication and that the rooms had been locked to prevent the men seeing things that might give away some of Barbie's games. I knew that when he tortured women he did it where there were toilets and basins. They were stripped of all their clothing, then they were purged and given medicine to make them vomit. He was one of Himmler's 'picked men', and as inhuman as his master.

15

Cyanide in my Shoe

I came straight back to England, and the Major and I tried to work out a plan to get me into the hotel. We discussed and discarded several; the risks were too great and the chances of success too slight. In the end the Major thought I had the best idea. My plan was to arrive at Lyon station as if I had got off the train from Paris. I would appear to be a stranger to Lyon, would find my way to the hotel and ask to see the Englishman. I could say that I was an old friend of the family and had a message from his mother. When and if I managed to interview him alone, I would try to get the required information from him.

I would pretend to be taking up a post as a school teacher in Pau, in the Basses-Pyrénées. I would not need to go to Paris as Jacques could obtain a rail ticket from Paris to Pau, bearing the right date, from his friends in the ticket offices. He could also supply me with a pass to leave Paris for the South. It would bear a forged signature and false information, but it would look quite authentic as Jacques was able to get hold of blank identity cards and work papers. I never knew how he did this; I was just grateful for his help.

I could say that I was breaking my journey in Lyon for a couple of days because I did not start work in Pau until the Monday following. The big question in my mind was, if I succeeded in making contact with the man and he was not willing to cooperate, what would I do? I put this to the Major. He said simply, 'You dispose of him.'

I was speechless. I suppose I had always known at the back of my mind that the day would come when I was asked to kill someone, but it was not until now that I fully realised it. It was one thing to kill an enemy in battle, quite another to commit cold-blooded murder. I knew that my group had killed Germans, but for me it was different. I was a doctor. I had taken an oath to preserve human life.

The Major was watching me and when I remained silent he said, 'Have a drink.' He poured out a brandy, and when I had gulped it down he said, 'It has to be faced, Jay Bee.'

I knew he was right. I had always dreaded this moment, but had put the thought out of my mind. He offered me a second brandy, which I accepted and drank in a more ladylike manner.

'Feeling better now?' he inquired.

I nodded.

'You have accepted the details of this assignment so far?'

The details of the assignment! A nice cosy way to talk of murder. I nodded again, but to myself I was saying, 'I will not kill. I will pray that in some way it can be averted.'

Churchill approved the plan. He thought it was simple enough to succeed, but insisted that I should wear a light uniform under my civilian dress on this occasion; I would also, for the first time, be carrying a capsule of cyanide. If I should be unfortunate enough to be captured by the Wehrmacht or the Vichy Police, my uniform, even when worn underneath civilian clothes, would be respected and I would be accorded the treatment agreed to under the Geneva Convention for military prisoners. As a civilian captive I would be considered to be a spy or a member of the Resistance and could be tortured and sent to a concentration camp or shot. The Gestapo, however, made no such distinction, and if they were my captors I would have to take my cyanide capsule to avoid torture.

Churchill told the Major to arrange that I should have every possible help as this was the most dangerous assignment I had yet undertaken. He asked if I had been told what was at stake. The Major said that he was confident I would carry out the mission, however distasteful.

I put in, 'How shall I be certain whether or not the man is a traitor?' To kill a traitor was bad enough , but to kill an innocent man...

That, I was told, was a decision that only I could make. Appearances were against him, but if I saw him alone I would soon know. I was to say straight out that I had arrived from England and wanted information on the type of concrete the Germans were using. If this story was accepted without query, I could be sure he was a traitor. If, on the other hand, he questioned me, and said it was impossible for me to have come from England, it would mean that he had little contact with events and was being used by the Germans. It would then be up to me to deal with the situation.

'Major,' said Churchill, 'be sure you cover all contingencies. We don't want to lose her. And you, Jay Bee - I can only wish you a safe and successful trip. And remember - never be taken alive!'

I was very quiet on my way back to the flat, and the Major left me to my thoughts. He came in, and over sandwiches, coffee and brandy we went over the whole plan again. It was to be a short assignment. After getting away from Lyon, I would be picked up by a plane at midnight on Saturday; five hours would be all I needed for success or failure and we would have only eight to fifteen minutes for the pick-up. If the pick-up plane did not see any signals it would return to England. It would have a pilot who was unknown to me so we would have to be given very clear signals. My usual pilot would take me in, in time to be in Lyon by eight o'clock in the evening, and my special group would meet me at the landing-ground.

As it was October, I could easily wear a light uniform under my tweed suit - consisting merely of a khaki blouse and skirt, and I would wear an identity disk on a chain round my neck. I wore a silk scarf (made in Paris) like a cravat, so that it hid my blouse; my suit was brown and beige tweed, my hat of light felt and fashionable in Paris in the 1930s. My large handbag was also fashionable at that period, and would hold my equipment; I was not going to stay, so I would travel light. My cigarette lighter was, on adjustment, a compass, and I also had a compass watch.

I wore a pair of former golf shoes. They were of fawn suede, by Jaeger, and had been made in Paris before the war to match a camel-hair suit. The soles and heels were very thick and made of corrugated rubber crêpe. A piece of rubber from one of the heels had been slightly loosened, and it was in this cavity that I carried my cyanide capsule. It was undetectable. I was very content to have this capsule as far away from my mouth as possible. I had seen rats die of cyanide poisoning and it was not a pretty sight. I knew, however, that I would swallow it if circumstances arose in which death was the only answer. I would never be taken alive.

As I wanted to visit the hotel on a Saturday, it meant leaving England late on Friday. Jules was contacted and the rendezvous arranged. Nearly all V.I.P.s and S.O.E. left this country from Tangmere by this time, but the Lysander in which I flew was kept at Tempsford, where there was a fighter squadron, and I still took off and arrived back there. The R.E. major escorted me to the airfield. As we drove through the now familiar countryside it was a really lovely autumn night; the stars were shining and the moon had risen, and I felt a little sad. The visits to the airfield had become a part of my life, and I wondered whether I would ever be taking this journey again.

When we arrived at Tempsford the Major was waiting with a Group Captain whom he introduced to me. The Major was quiet and the R.E. major looked worried. My pilot arrived and greeted me with, 'Hullo! The Unknown Woman again. How are you this fine evening?' His unfailing perkiness was an antidote to the gloom of those we were leaving behind at Tempsford. Although we never exchanged more than a few brief words, there seemed to be a bond between us. I have always had the feeling that airmen and sailors, because of the loneliness of the vast spaces that surround them, are different from other people; perhaps because they find themselves nearer to God.

Once when we were waiting at Tempsford my pilot told me he would not be a bomber pilot at any price. For a fighter pilot the odds were fairly even; he could not bear to think of his bombs killing innocent people. He was a coward at heart, he said, and admired Bomber Command pilots and crew; he felt they all hated the job but had the guts to carry on with it.

'You're sure you're satisfied with the plan, Jay Bee?' said the Major anxiously. This was a nice time to ask! There would not be much sense in changing my mind now. If I had known all that lay ahead of me on this assignment, I might have done just that and opted out. However, I knew the Major was just making conversation because we were all under a strain. I said yes, I was satisfied. The R.E. major looked very serious as he wished me good luck. The Major managed a smile and said, 'I'll see you on Sunday, Jay Bee.' He almost whispered the words. I had never seen him show so much emotion. As we taxied off he blew me a kiss. It was horribly like a farewell gesture, I thought. When we finally took off for France after a stop for refuelling I wondered if I had seen England for the last time, but I was in a philosophical mood. What was to be would be.

The time passed quickly and when I heard the engine turned off I knew the pilot was going to glide in. The wood at the side of the field where my men were waiting showed up well. We cleared it, skimming the tree-trops, and then from the pilot, 'Out!' I was on the ground and he was away. The men ran towards me and we went into the wood. Jules had a motor-cycle and I rode pillion to our next stop. This was a village near Lyon, and about an hour later the other three caught up with us there. Friends of Jules lived in the village - obviously the men of the family were Maquisards - and we were to stay with them until it was time to go into Lyon. They gave us plenty of food, and one of the women of the house had made some fruit juice which was ripe for drinking. I enjoyed it very much.

The Paris train was due to arrive at about 8 p.m. so there was plenty of time to brief my group. They had arranged for one of the men who, in the guise of plumbers, had inspected the hotel from inside, to come here to see me. I had already had a detailed report from them, but they had been rather excited, and I wanted to be sure that I had an accurate picture. How long exactly was the cul-de-sac? How far down it were the two windows that they were sure belonged to a Ladies' Room? He told me they were nearer to the entrance than to the blind end. I was relieved to hear this. If I escaped this way, I did not want to find myself trapped in a blind alley.

When Jules had taken the man back to his home I went over the plan with my 'Specials'. I gave them all the details, but said nothing about the information I wanted from the Englishman. Jules gave me my rail ticket, identity card and the permit - the work papers and ration cards were not there; Jacques had not been able to get them in time. I said it was not important; I would say that I had sent them on to the Headmistress of the school where I was expected on Monday. I might not even be asked for them.

We arranged to get to the station, just before 8 p.m. Once I was in the station the men would wait nearby, so that after the train from Paris arrived they would meet me outside. I told them that I would go straight to the hotel from the station and ask to see the Englishman. Two of them were to wait near or under the windows in the cul-de-sac, the other two were to be in front of the hotel as near as possible under the window of the Englishman's room. They knew the location from a drawing the 'workmen' had made and which I had personally destroyed.

There was, of course, a good chance that I might be turned away from the hotel. If I did get in, the men were to give me an hour at most. The two men in front of the hotel were to watch the windows of the Englishman's room. If I was in it and found myself in trouble I would try to move the curtain so that a slit of light showed - black-out was in force here, though not as strictly as in the coastal region. The curtain covered tall casement windows. If they saw it move they were to get in by way of the balconies.

I told them that I had the means with me to end my life, and would use it if necessary. If the worst happened, then Jules would radio 'mission failed' and either meet the plane at midnight and send it back or, if he judged it dangerous for the plane to land, not signal it in. The pilot would not land unless he saw the correct signal.

When we reached the station we found a great deal of activity: S.S., Gestapo, Vichy Police and a number of Militia were posted outside it. 'Looks as though they were expecting trouble,' remarked Pierre. Jules reminded us that it was Saturday, and perhaps an important German was visiting for the week-end. This often happened. Generals on leave and other officials considered Lyon a very pleasant city - plenty of food and brothels. They knew they could enjoy a respite here.

Pierre said the Gestapo did not meet important Germans, only S.S. or Gestapo personnel or escapees. For whatever reason they were there, I had to get past them unobserved, or my whole plan of arriving along with the passengers from Paris would fail before it had begun. My men said they would create a diversion. They started a noisy brawl and two of them ran towards the Germans with the other two chasing them. At the same time I dashed past and into the station - and so did several other people! I heard angry shouts, but they were not directed at us. The running men had attracted all attention to themselves. I hid on the station till the train came in, and then joined the stream of passengers as they emerged.

The railway staff were not collecting tickets - this job was being done by the Gestapo, while the Vichy Police stood by. Sometimes the Gestapo took over and collected the tickets, as they were doing now, or watched tickets being collected, for no apparent reason. They were constantly on the look-out for escapees. My turn arrived and I showed my ticket for Pau. The officer looked hard at me and told me I should have gone on to Toulouse. 'Why have you come to Lyon?' he demanded.

I told him about my new post at the school, starting on Monday, and the friend in Paris who had a son working in Lyon and had asked me to visit him. I had never been in Lyon before, and thought it a good opportunity to see the city. The officer asked for the man's name and address. I gave the name of the hotel and the street, and explained that though the man had an

English name, he had been naturalised for years. His mother was French and a widow. He asked me if I intended to stay the night in Lyon, and I said I would if I could get a room. Perhaps I could stay in the same hotel as my friend's son. It occurred to me as I spoke that I carried no suit-case; but if the question arose my large handbag could easily pass as hand-luggage for one night - provided it was not searched.

The officer stared hard at me, but I did not flinch. 'Supposing you can't get a room?' he asked.

'Surely there must be plenty of hotels in Lyon?' I said.

One of the Vichy Police who heard me nodded. 'I believe there is a midnight train to Toulouse?' I said, appealing to him. He nodded again. Then the Gestapo officer spoke the words I most dreaded: 'Your papers, madame.'

I did not hesitate. I opened my bag and took my identity card and pass, and launched into the explanation that my ration cards and work papers had been sent to the Headmistress to check that they were in order. I said the name of the school was the Ecole Normale. (There was in fact such a school in Pau. The Headmistress worked for the Resistance and had been warned about me in case enquiries were made there.) He studied the identity card and keep looking me up and down while I waited patiently, trying to look nonchalant. I was more than relieved when he handed them back to me with my railway ticket and said curtly, 'You may proceed.' I thanked him and left the station.

I walked on towards the hotel and was rejoined by the men. They told me that the Vichy Police had arrested them on a 'drunk and disorderly' charge and escorted them from the station. The two who had arrested them were friends, and had immediately released them. We had all come out of the affair very well, and I should have been pleased that the first obstacle was successfully surmounted, but I was feeling quite the reverse. In the past when I sensed danger I felt a tingling at the nape of my neck and my hair seemed to rise. I felt it then, and told the men that I was worried, but did not know why.

'Why not cancel the whole affair?' said Pierre at once. 'I think it's madness!'

I said no, we would carry on as planned. Having had the warning of some unforeseen danger I would be very alert. It was too late to turn back now. They took up their positions, and I entered the hotel.

16

A Package for the Major

I entered the hotel. According to my men's report, there were no civilians in the hotel except the Englishman, but the man at the reception desk wore civilian clothes. I asked for the Englishman, and I was given the number of his room, twenty-seven, and told that it was on the second floor. I was relieved to find it was the same room my men had told me of - at least Pierre and Antoine would be waiting below the right window. All the same, I would have been happier if there had been more fuss about letting me go up to it. I was always suspicious when things seemed too easy. Had I been recognised? Was this a trap? I was not really surprised that some of the Germans standing about were from the group I had seen at the station. However, as I was telling the receptionist the same story I had told there, they had - as far as I knew - no reason to doubt its truth.

The Germans took no particular notice of me, but I had a strong desire to run up the stairs and out of sight. I controlled this impulse and went up slowly. I thought, 'Supposing there are Gestapo in the man's room waiting for me?' I wondered whether, if this were so, the adjacent rooms would be open so that I could dash into one of them and take my capsule, or even perhaps have a chance to escape by way of the balconies.

I came to the door of room number twenty-seven. I knocked and a voice invited me to come in. I flung the door wide open so that I could see if the man was alone and if there were other doors opening into the room which might conceal witnesses. He was alone, and I could see no other door. I came in and as I closed the door behind me I noticed that the key was in the lock, so I leant back against it and with one hand behind me I locked it and took out the key.

The man did not notice. He was looking at my face and I heard myself saying, in English, 'I have come from England. I am looking for information on cements and I understand that you are an expert. Will you help me?'

His reaction to this was at the heart of the whole matter, and all my senses were alert to interpret it. Astonishment, incredulity, hope, alarm - for himself and for me also - any or all of these would be natural if he was an unwilling prisoner. He showed none of them. 'Yes, certainly,' he said coolly, and turned aside from me. 'Wait a moment and I'll get my papers.'

I was afraid to let him turn away. He might well be going to summon help; I started to talk and went on talking to keep him there. 'There is no hurry,' I said. 'They don't suspect me. I am sure you'd like to hear what we are doing in England and how I come to be in Lyon.'

He seemed quite at ease, and agreed that there was plenty of time. An unlikely suggestion under the circumstances! But he showed no real curiosity about my arrival or about the situation in England. I remembered what I had been told: 'If he accepts you without query, you may be sure he is a traitor.' There was no doubt in my mind. His whole attitude betrayed him. He was ready to let me talk, to linger here in danger, confident of his own safety. It was clear that I would get no useful information from him here. But if he could be got away ...

I continued to talk, as if I took his interest for granted, and as I talked I walked slowly towards the window, pretended to trip over the hem of the curtain, and moved it slightly so that a ray of light was exposed. I did not stop talking. I was telling him how helpful his information would be to us ...

It happened so quickly that even I was taken by surprise. I had hardly moved the curtain before the window was thrust open and Pierre and Antoine were in the room. I think they must have been already on the balcony. I never had time to ask them. The man opened his mouth to shout but no sound came. Pierre was upon him in a flash and knocked him out cold. Antoine caught him as he fell - even though the building was solid, a loud thud was not desirable at that moment.

From then on all was done in haste, but in almost complete silence. I told the men they must get their prisoner out of here and to the field where the plane was landing at midnight. They assured me that they could manage him, dead weight though he was, and that I would find it quite easy to follow them by climbing from this balcony to the one below and then to the street. I shook my head. I was sure it would not be long before some of the

Germans came to the room, and I had thought of a way of bluffing them and holding them off for a time while the others got clear away with the unconscious man. There were very few people about in the streets at this hour, and no civilian would dare to interfere if he saw a man being abducted. It was not an uncommon sight. Our chief danger was from the Vichy Police, but in Lyon many of them were our friends. I told them to go to Vincent's garage, get a car from him, and take the man to the rendezvous. They were to leave Jules and Georges where they were, in the cul-de-sac, as I meant to escape by that route. If I did not turn up at the field they must tie the man up and get him aboard the plane, then disappear as fast as possible. They were distressed at leaving me, but did as I asked.

I waited until they were safely down into the street with their captive - Pierre was as agile as a cat and Antoine very strong, so they accomplished the descent without difficulty. The black-out was in our favour. The streets were dark and all windows curtained or shuttered. No alarm was raised, so I proceeded to put my plan into action. I transferred the contents of my handbag to my pockets, took the capsule from my shoe and slipped it into my coat cuff where I could reach it quickly if the need arose. Then, leaving my hat, gloves and empty handbag in the room, I gently unlocked the door and went out, relocking the door behind me and pocketing the key. I was just in time, because four Gestapo officers had reached the top of the stairs and I was quite certain they were on their way to room twenty-seven. I turned back towards the door - they could not see from there that it was shut - and said loudly, as if I were speaking to the man inside, 'I won't be long!'

As I went towards the stairs the officers stood in my way. I recognised two of them - they travelled with Himmler as part of his bodyguard, and I wondered if that meant he was visiting Lyon at the present time. One of them inquired, 'Did you find your friend?' so I knew that they had been told about me. 'Oh yes, thank you', I said, 'and he has asked me to stay the night.'

They seemed surprised at this, and one of them asked me where I was going. 'Downstairs,' I said, 'to inform the receptionist that I'm staying. I shall have to sign the register and fill in the particulars.'

'You seem to know all the regulations, madame.'

'Naturally,' I said. 'I live in Paris, in the Occupied Zone, and I obey orders. I suppose it's just the same here, though it's Unoccupied?'

They still looked a little puzzled, but I felt that they had accepted the situation as I had no hat, gloves or handbag with me. They stood aside, and I was praying that they would follow me downstairs. If even one of them went to the room and found it locked and empty, I was finished. I started to go down. I did not dare look round, but heard them all four behind me. My right hand was straying towards my left cuff. Thankfully I let it fall to my side.

As I approached the reception desk I saw that the civilian man receptionist had been replaced by a girl - blonde, beautiful, one of the two who were always near Himmler. They were girls of the New Order and future Nordic Empire. Himmler was definitely in Lyon, then - perhaps here, in the hotel, at this moment. The thought was not encouraging. I explained the situation to the girl and she placed a book and the usual form in front of me and offered me a pen. I took it from her and was about to fill in the form, but suddenly put the pen down, smiled at the girl and asked her if it would be all right to visit the Ladies' Room first. She pointed along the corridor. The 'plumbers' had been right. I remembered the lay-out of the ground floor as they had described it. The Ladies' Room - or so-called 'store room' - which they had not been allowed to inspect was at the end of the corridor to the right of the reception desk.

I walked slowly along, once more overcoming a desire to run, and when I reached the room I tried the handle of the door with trepidation. What would I do if it was locked? It opened easily. I went in and very quickly shut the door, drew the bolt across, and looked about me. The men had done their work well. The two windows which faced on to the cul-de-sac were there as they had reported. I examined them. The men had said that no fastening was visible from the outside, but this was not surprising as they were frosted and completely opaque. But now I was horrified to see that there was no latch on the inside either. They were completely sealed. There was no question of my going back, as the Gestapo were in the corridor. I was trapped here and they knew it. Even now they might have discovered that the bird had flown from room twenty-seven.

This was the moment of decision. Either I got out of this death-trap now, this very minute, or I took the capsule from my cuff and bit on it. Death would be quick. Churchill had said, 'Never be taken alive.' He would understand. All this went through my mind like a flash as I studied those horrible blind windows. I thought of my parting with the Major at Tempsford. 'See you on Sunday!' I was not beaten yet. Surely my knowledge of Karate, in which I had been so meticulously trained for the purpose of killing, could be put to use to save my own life. The glass looked thick and strong, it was perhaps double, but the windows were not barred, and somewhere outside them two of my most loyal men were waiting for me. If I had to die, at least I would die fighting. I drew myself into a Karate position. My lungs were full. I knew that I had only forty seconds. I went head first through one of the windows.

I went so quickly and with such force that the window shattered and I fell, upside down, into the astonished arms of Georges. He was so startled that he hung on to me and I thought he was never going to turn me right side up! It can have been for only a few seconds that I remained in this inelegant position, but seconds can feel like hours at such a time. Eventually I found myself standing on my own feet, completely unharmed. There was not a scratch on me. I recovered my breath. In spite of the noise of broken glass we appeared to be still alone in the alley. I said, 'Let's get to Vincent's!' We dashed into the street and hurried to the garage. As we went along I gave Georges and Jules a brief account of what had happened.

When we arrived at Vincent's garage I asked if Pierre and Antoine had called. He said that Pierre had been and he had let him have a small van. I explained that we must now have a car as we needed to get away from Lyon immediately. I told him I had escaped from the Gestapo hotel and that there would be a search for me, probably a full-scale search, so he must warn all groups in the area. Vincent took this quite calmly, merely saying, 'God, what luck you came in time to warn me. I have four escapees here waiting to go on an escape route - British air crew who have been on the run for over four months. I'll get them out at once.'

Vincent was a very cool type and fooled the Germans time after time. He mixed with the Vichy Police and some of the Militia; he was never suspected. On one occasion he was hiding some explosives in a vegetable patch behind his house. Two German soldiers saw him at his work and asked him what he was doing. 'Can't you see?' he said. 'I'm planting out cabbages. Care to give me a hand? I have plenty more plants to put in.' The soldiers laughed and went away. Vincent had two hand grenades in his coat pocket and under each cabbage plant there were explosives!

I explained to Vincent why we needed a car as well as the van that Pierre had taken, and promised that the men would return them both by morning in case the Germans came to check on his cars. I asked about his escapees. He said it was all right, he had another van and would take them south to a safe house where they could be put on to the escape route over the Pyrenees.

When we arrived at the field where the plane was to pick me up we found Pierre and Antoine there. They were delighted to see us. The prisoner was lying on the ground, bound hand and foot and still unconscious. When I told them how I had escaped Pierre said gloomily, 'It's not over yet. The Germans will be furious. The blow to their pride will make them more vicious than ever. Anyway, *you* are safe. That's the main thing.'

'We are all safe,' I said, 'so cheer up. We have got our man and he's a very valuable catch.'

I broke the news to them then that I did not intend to go back with the plane. I had been thinking about it, and had come to the conclusion that the combined weights of the captive and myself would make things very difficult, possibly dangerous, for the pilot. I have mentioned earlier that the Lysander was essentially a two-seater, though it could carry more weight in an emergency. This was, however, no longer strictly true. Bigger tanks had now replaced the original ones, which meant that the planes, with this additional fuel, could fly further into enemy territory. It also meant that they were heavier and less manoeuvrable and an extra load would make taking off and low flying a very risky business. When I explained this to my group, Jules suggested getting rid of the man - who, fortunately for him, was still unconscious and did not hear this discussion of his fate. Having managed to fulfil my assignment without taking a life, I did not intend that life to be sacrificed now. I told Jules and the others that this was a very important prisoner, holding information that was vital to the Allies, and he must be got to England alive. I would make my way to Tarbes by my escape route. I would be quite safe.

We heard the engines of the plane and gave the signals as arranged. I had put a coded note into the prisoner's pocket and had written another message, not in code, for the pilot to give to the Major at Tempsford. The plane glided in, and when I saw the pilot any doubts I may still have had about returning with him were now resolved. He was a very large, powerfully-built man, much heavier than my usual pilot. I said that a man would be going back to England in my place. 'I was told that the pick-up was a woman,' he said doubtfully. 'You fit the description.' I asked him to read the note I was sending with him for the Major. My men were meanwhile bundling their captive into the plane and tying him securely to the seat beside the pilot. If he recovered whilst airborne he would be unable to move. The pilot was very sensible. He just said, 'O.K., I take your word for it. Thanks for the note.' He glanced at his trussed-up passenger and said laconically, 'That one will be no trouble. If he wakes up and gets nasty I'll knock him out again.' Then he was away.

I felt dazed. I seemed to have lived through a lifetime, yet it had all happened in less than four hours. I think the others felt as I did, for all five of us sat for a moment, wordless, at the corner of the field. Then Jules remarked, 'Was it a dream or did it really happen?'

'It happened,' I said. I was conscious only of a great thankfulness. I had kept my promise to myself not to kill, and the responsibility was no longer mine. I pictured the Lysander on its flight home to England without me. I could not help smiling to myself as I imagined the Major's expression when he met it at Tempsford and received, in place of myself, a package neatly tied up by my Maquisards.

We roused ourselves and discussed our plans. There was no time to lose as the search for us would be well under way. I asked Pierre to warn some of the brothel girls that there was a hunt on, as they knew a great many of the Resistance and could pass on the warning. Georges said, 'You can bet anything that Vincent has already put out the warning, but we'll all do what we can.' I asked Jules to phone the school at Pau and inform them that I was on the Escape Route, and to tell them to deny any knowledge of me if the Gestapo should make inquiries. I also asked him to get a message through to England as soon as possible and say that all was well with me, but that we would be out of contact until they heard from me. We seldom used radio in case the Bletchley Code Breakers became too clever and picked up our messages. The Secret Circle was unknown to anyone outside it and must remain so.

The men were loath for me to go on the run alone and wanted to come with me. They were prepared to sacrifice their jobs for this. They were not married, so did not have families dependent on them. I told them it was far more important that they should remain in their jobs. They were doing valuable work where they were, intercepting communications and organising sabotage, they would be put to good use when the Allies invaded France to liberate her. 'That day is a long way off,' said Pierre, the pessimist; but I knew that he would do all that he could to bring it nearer. They were worried about my choosing to go in the direction of Pau, but I said that I was sure the Germans would look everywhere else but there, as they had seen my rail ticket for Pau, and would expect me to avoid it like the plague. I reminded them to get the two cars back before morning to Vincent's garage, and told Jules I would get in touch as soon as I reached Tarbes.

They all looked very sad and I realised how much I had become part of their lives, and they of mine. It came over me once again that in this strange comradeship we shared they had never once embarrassed me, though they were men and I the only woman. They were never anything but courteous and considerate. As I said 'au revoir' I put my right hand out to shake hands, but each of them in turn, without the least trace of self-consciousness, took my hand and kissed it. I wanted to hug them, but I turned away and left them gazing after me as I started on my long walk to the Basses-Pyrénées.

17

The Long Walk

My destination was the last safe house on my route, a villa on the outskirts of Tarbes in the Basses-Pyrénées. It was owned by Portuguese friends of the Major, some of the many who helped us although they were officially neutral. I knew I faced a formidable and hazardous journey, but it was my only chance of evading capture. I must get as far away as possible from the Lyon area. Speed was important, but even so I felt I would be much safer on foot than using any sort of transport. I was sure the Germans would not consider the possibility of my escaping in this way. They would almost certainly concentrate on trains leaving Lyon, but having so recently interrogated me at the station and examined my ticket, they would never imagine me crazy enough to make for Pau.

No one, not even my most trusted friends, knew the route I intended to take, but it was firmly imprinted on my mind. I knew the area well from pre-war days and was familiar not only with the National routes but also with the smaller country roads, and I decided to keep to the latter, avoiding villages and farms. To this day I cannot explain why I did not make some provision for food on my journey. I suppose events had crowded one upon another so rapidly that any preparations for departure seemed of little importance. The question of food had worried my men, but I had assured them that I could live off the land. My main thoughts were that I must get out of the region without delay, that my group must scatter and not appear to be connected with me, and that all underground cells which might be endangered should be warned to lie low.

On several previous assignments I had been provided with vitamin tablets as emergency rations but on this occasion none had been issued, because I was expected to return at midnight on Saturday. The possibility of removing the cement expert, whether willing or unwilling, from under the noses of the Gestapo had not even been mooted - it was too fantastic. If he had been willing to cooperate, I would have got the necessary information and left at once; if he proved traitor my instructions were to dispose of him. Instead, I had acted on my own initiative, so it was up to me to get myself out of trouble.

I decided to get into a steady, regular walking rhythm and continue without pause through the hours of darkness, and if possible lie hidden and rest up by day. In this way I would conserve my energy to the best advantage. I carried with me a compass watch, compass powder compact and compass cigarette case, so I was well equipped to keep to my route, and the cyanide capsule (now back in my shoe) also gave me confidence.

It was a beautiful, clear October night and the moon, now riding high in the sky, provided light enough for me to find my way quite easily. There was no one about at this hour and the only sounds in the quietness of the French countryside were those of my own regular footsteps as my shoes crunched the first fallen leaves of autumn, and the occasional rustle of some small nocturnal animal scurrying away into the undergrowth. As I moved further away from the danger area I began to relax and enjoy my solitary night walk. The air was clean and crisp and I felt invigorated. This was reality. The hectic events of the last twenty-four hours were already as unreal as a dream.

As dawn broke I thought it was time to begin looking for a place to hide during the day. Fortunately the season of the year was to my advantage, for the days were growing shorter as the nights lengthened. As I walked my mind was occupied by planning what I should eat to keep myself alive. Eventually I came upon a small copse near a running stream and decided to make this my first stopping place. I drank from the clear, cold water and then washed myself and feeling pleasantly refreshed began to look about for food. I found some mushrooms which I ate and enjoyed, and some edible weeds which, though not so appetising, would help to sustain me; but at this stage I was not feeling very hungry.

The next necessity was a place to hide until dark, so I looked about until I found some thick bushes and pushed my way in among them. Sitting here, I was well concealed but could peer out if I heard anyone approaching. It so happened that I was not disturbed, and I remained there quite snugly for the rest of the day. I managed to doze off from time to time, so I was feeling fairly fresh when the light began to fade and it was time to think of leaving my hiding place. After satisfying my personal needs and taking a final drink from the stream I set out on the next stage of my journey.

The weather was still fine and quite mild for the time of year, for which I was thankful, but towards early morning it became chilly and my hands were cold. I missed my hat too - when you are used to wearing one your head is sensitive to the cold. I wished I had had enough sense to borrow a beret from Jules, who always wore one when he was not in his Inspector's uniform, but it was pointless to wish now. However, I could have been much worse off. I was wearing warm clothing and very stout shoes, and I also had the extra warmth of my service uniform underneath my tweed suit. As a precaution against being shot as a spy I hoped it would be unnecessary, but as protection from the chill of autumn it was a welcome bonus.

As before, the moon rose to light my way, and as the sky grew lighter I found myself near a small farm. I was still uncomfortably close to Lyon so I approached with great caution, but there was no sign of life and all was quiet, except for the officious crowing of a cockerel proclaiming to the world at large that dawn was about to break, so I ventured near one of the outhouses. Here I was in luck. I found some carrots and small potatoes, took as many as I could carry, and chewed at the cleanest-looking carrot as I walked on looking for water. Soon I came to a fresh spring in which I could wash my precious vegetables and take another refreshing drink.

As I washed my face and hands in the cold spring water I was conscious of the silence and stillness of the early morning. There was not even the sound of a cockerel now, not a bird was stirring. It was a friendly silence, like a protective cloak wrapped about me. I felt at peace as I continued on at the steady pace to which I had grown accustomed, checking my direction from time to time with a compass to make sure I did not stray off course. Presently, as the light grew brighter, I came to a small village at the edge of which was a wooden hut. As there was no one about as yet, and I must lose no opportunity of acquiring food or other useful stores, I risked exploring it.

I crept up to the door and peeped through a crack. Inside was a nanny goat tethered with her kid beside her, so I quickly slipped in and sat down on the hay. The hay was warm and dry, and the tangy, milky smell of the goats was not unpleasant. My dearest wish at that moment was just to relax and stay there, but it was impossible; at any minute the owner might appear. The animals seemed as pleased to have my company as I was to be with them.

The young one snuggled up to me. This spontaneous demonstration of trust to a complete stranger gave me an unexpected feeling of comfort. Nationality had no meaning for this affectionate little creature. How much more sense he showed than the human race.

In the hut was a pail with drinking water for the goats, but I did not touch it, for the pail was very dirty and in any case I had recently quenched my thirst at the spring. There were also several large cabbage leaves lying around. In one corner lay a quite clean-looking canvas bag. I helped myself to it and put some of the hay into it together with the cleanest cabbage leaves and the remainder of my carrots and potatoes. It was a most useful find. I longed to get some milk from the nanny goat. I had milked a goat before, and could have managed it by catching the milk in one cupped hand, but I dared not try as I had once contracted Maltese fever from infected goat's milk. Reluctantly I said goodbye to mother and son and went in search of a more secluded place in which to hide and rest till nightfall.

It was becoming dangerously light now, and it was high time I went to ground. I saw a wood which might provide cover and made my way towards it. Some distance away two early-rising workers were busy in a field, but luckily they were intent on their task and did not raise their heads. I was relieved to find that the wood was thick with trees; it was just what I needed for my refuge. I actually found a hollow tree with an opening just big enough for me to squeeze through, so I climbed inside - after making my presence known to any animal occupant that might have had the same views as myself on desirable residences. The canvas bag stuffed with hay made a comfortable pillow for my back and head, and I fell asleep almost immediately in these unaccustomed surroundings. I must have slept solidly all day after a night's exercise in the fresh air, for I do not remember anything disturbing me until I woke to find that it was quite dark. The long sleep had done me good, but I could not afford to waste time and crawled out of my hole to start my third night's march.

Once again the night was clear and dry and the stars were very bright. I set my compass and walked on. I had begun to talk to myself. I had the strange feeling that I was alone in the world, and hearing the sound of my own voice was some comfort. I willed myself not think of England or of friends and family there, and concentrated on my objective - the safe house in Tarbes.

The days and nights that followed are blurred one into another in memory, yet each one had its own character; each night had its own hopes and fears, its own small triumphs and disappointments; each day had its own hiding-place, some cold and cramped, others surprisingly snug and comfortable; some broken by false alarms, others undisturbed and blessed with sleep.

When the raw carrots and potatoes and the cabbage leaves were gone my staple diet was edible fungi. I found several varieties besides field mushrooms. The best was a purple one which the French chop up and use in salads. They are much more knowledgeable about fungi than the majority of the English. I also found edible roots and weeds; there was a type of large-leaved sorrel which is also used in salads. On good days berries provided a welcome dessert. All these helped to ease my hunger, and I was glad that I had a good knowledge of plants and fungi; but I realised that on this restricted diet my energy was flagging, and though I still kept up a steady pace I was not walking as fast as when I started out. However, so long as I passed plenty of streams and could drink fresh water my condition was reasonably good.

Sometimes I could hear traffic on the National roads, but I still kept to the byways and avoided all contact with people. As I walked on night after night I was increasingly conscious of my solitude, but although I was so alone I did not feel lonely. During my life circumstances had forced me to spend so much time alone that I had learnt to appreciate solitude, and I was now thankful that I had had this experience. I thought of how fastidious I had been before the war - how fussy I had always been about bathrooms and toilets. I had possessed a lovely bathroom in my Paris flat and now I was living like a gypsy - my diet was gathered from the fields and hedgerows; my toilet was the woods and streams. I began to think about the luxurious bath I was going to indulge in if I reached civilisation again. The water would be very hot and I would use masses of perfume! How I would revel in it.

When I left my hiding-place on the ninth night I found that I was walking much more slowly; moreover I was unable to find any water. At one time I saw a vineyard in the distance and was very tempted to go there, but in spite of my weakness and thirst I dared not take the risk of meeting people. The character of the country had changed as I covered the miles, and this waterless stretch of land had come when my body was most in need of water. I plodded on, eating fungi for sustenance and chewing grass, hoping to absorb some moisture. I thought of all the delicious meals I had enjoyed in the past, and the saliva began to flow, easing the dryness of my mouth and tongue. I thought nostalgically of all those streams from which I had drunk on my journey. At times I had needed to cross them, but fortunately they were never too deep and I took off my shoes and stockings, then afterwards dried my feet with leaves. What a joy that would be now.

I hid as usual during daylight hours, but it was an effort to start walking again when darkness fell. At one time I began to feel that I was not alone. Was I being followed? I stopped dead in my tracks and listened intently; all was silent, except that now and then a dry leaf detached itself from a tree and fell gently to the ground at my feet. My hearing had become very acute. There were no footsteps to be heard but my own as I set off again. I was letting my imagination get the better of me.

On the eleventh night I still had not found water. If only it would rain! I would not complain about muddy tracks or the chill and discomfort of wet clothes; but the long dry spell obstinately persisted. My mouth was dry and I could no longer make saliva. My lips were cracked, and when I applied lipstick, hoping to relieve the dryness, they began to smart. I knew that I was dehydrating, and my sparse diet was not sufficient to meet the energy I had had to use up in walking. The moisture in my body was fast disappearing; and there was still no water to be found.

I seemed to have been walking for a very short time when I slowed down and then stopped, and however hard I tried I could not move. The moon had not yet risen, but brilliant stars lit up the sky and shed a faint radiance over the field beside which I stood. I gazed about me like a mortally wounded animal seeking cover where it may die in privacy. I was at the end of my endurance. I could not take another step, but I was out in the open. It was imperative that I should not be found alive, yet I was rooted to the spot. There was only one course open to me - now was the time to take my cyanide capsule. I tried to bend down to take off my shoe and remove the capsule from its place of concealment in the thick rubber heel; I could not do it; I was completely paralysed and could not even bend down. Yet my brain was perfectly clear. I thought, 'Soon I must fall down. I cannot die standing up.' I prayed for help - to be able to lie down and die quickly. I was not afraid; I just wanted the end to be quick.

Suddenly I saw that the night had become darker. The stars had disappeared, but I could see no clouds. My eyesight must be fading. I stood there in the darkness praying for death, and then the Miracle happened. Let doubters call it what they will; I can only call it a miracle, for it happened to me exactly as I describe it here:

I saw a cloud descending and coming towards me. It was a brilliant blue and it floated around me until I was completely encased in cloud. Then down through the cloud as if suspended from heaven a white line appeared. It was about four inches wide and came right down to touch the toe of my right foot, and my foot involuntarily moved on to it. I could move! What was happening? I moved my left foot, placing my heel in front of the right toe, and then I repeated the movement with my right foot and began walking in this way. My one thought was, 'I must keep on this white line.' Some force was compelling me. The blue cloud disappeared as suddenly as it had come and the stars shone out again, but the white line remained, stretching out in front of me. I continued to walk, heel to toe, along the line, not questioning where it was leading me. I had lost count of time and distance when, still on the line, I came to a small barn. The line continued on and I followed it inside, then fell down exhausted. I must have slept then, for I woke to find daylight streaming in, but I did not try to move. I just closed my eyes again as I felt so comfortable.

When I next woke up it was dark and I could see the stars shining through the open doorway. My mouth was miraculously full of saliva, which I swallowed. My mouth filled up again and I began to drink my own saliva. My lips were no longer dry and I did not feel hungry. I began to try to piece together the events that had brought me here, and I knew that I had had the great privilege of experiencing a miracle. The paralysis had prevented me from taking my own life by the use of my cyanide capsule, but what had followed was even more awe-inspiring. I have never been more sure of the presence of God than I was in that barn. I had always had great faith, but now I can say with truth and humility that I know God exists, and if one has sufficient faith in God and in the power of prayer one can always rely on help when it is most needed.

I was now quite prepared to continue walking, but I wondered if I was still on my route. I struck my lighter and looked at my compass and was delighted to find that I was heading in the right direction, and by looking at the stars I found that I was still on course. The canvas bag was lying in the barn, but I had no recollection of having carried it there. I remembered that the pocket handkerchief I was carrying became a map when dampened and I was able to do this with my own saliva, which was still plentiful. I made a note of the landmarks and minor roads. When I reached the Basque country the land would be flatter and I would need to be careful of the vineyards and small holdings.

As I left the barn my foot struck something soft just outside the door. I thought it might be a small animal so I stopped to investigate, but it was a piece of cloth with something wrapped in it. I took the little bundle back into the barn and struck my lighter for a closer look. The cloth was wrapped round some cheese, home-made bread and an apple. To me at that moment it was as if I gazed upon a banquet. I wondered if someone had seen me while I lay sleeping and had left food for me, or was it a forgotten lunch? Either way, I looked upon it as a gift. I put the cheese and bread into my canvas bag for a future meal and bit into the apple as I started to walk. It was ambrosia - it was the food of the gods! I have never since enjoyed eating anything as much as I did that apple.

As I walked on I felt that the terrain was different. Although the moon had waned the night was not really dark as the stars provided enough light for me to see by, and I realised that I was already in the Basque country. I must have walked for miles on that white line, guided along, I am quite convinced, by Divine power. I had not until then fully appreciated the direction in which I had been led when I had given up all hope of reaching my destination, and I felt very humble. I was not worthy of such help. I was very happy, and hummed a tune as I walked along. I realised that the tune was, 'I want to be happy'!

I longed for daylight to come so that I could see the countryside more clearly and get my bearings. Nearby I heard the welcome sound of rippling water. A stream! Although I had lost my desperate thirst I was glad to drink my fill and wash myself, taking plenty of time over it. My hair was a mess. I had mislaid my comb at some point and I attempted, not very successfully, to comb my hair with a twig. Suddenly I felt something hard in the breast pocket of my khaki uniform blouse and remembered that there was a very small comb tucked into it. I cannot describe the joy of this discovery. There is no better morale-booster than the ability to tidy one's hair.

As dawn approached I saw and heard signs of life. There were two men in the distance, and I could hear heavy vehicles on the National route. I wondered what kind they were, and as the noise continued I could identify it as a convoy; by the sound they were tanks or very heavy lorries. Then, by landmarks I knew very well, I saw that I was approaching the town of Pau. It was not the end of my journey, but it was near the end. There were friends not far away, and I had the strength to reach them. Had I really walked all those miles in twelve days ... or was it thirteen?

On the outskirts of the town I passed a shop and saw by the date on a newspaper that it was fourteen nights since I had left my men at the rendezvous. Then ahead of me, rising up through the shrouds of morning mist, I saw one of the most magnificent sights in the world - the great, jagged line of the Pyrénées, their high peaks crowned in glittering snow. I lifted my eyes to the hills and gave thanks for my preservation. I think that altogether I must have covered over 300 miles. I do not remember much after the Miracle and arriving at the barn.

18

The Blue-grey Austin

I had worn my clothes for fourteen days without a change. All the same, I reflected, I looked presentable enough to pass without remark in a town the size of Pau, now that there were people about in the streets. It was the hour when many of them were hurrying to work, and housewives were going out to the shops or to the market. My hair was tidy, thanks to the discovery of the small pocket comb. Fortunately my suit was made of tweed, which did not show wear and tear, and I had brushed it down before entering the town. I had also cleaned my shoes, and the canvas bag which I still carried would pass muster in wartime when all goods were in short supply and people were having to use make-shift substitutes. In fact I saw some women carrying obviously home-made bags which were not unlike mine. In a small village any stranger would have been noticed. Here I could fade into the crowd.

I reckoned that if the Germans had made enquiries about me here they would have done so much earlier, and would no longer be looking out for me. I wanted to avoid the main roads as there seemed to be great deal of military traffic there, and it would not be easy to find a quiet route to Tarbes or safe hiding-places as I was now in a more thickly populated region. It seemed to me, therefore, that my best plan was to go straight to the station and take a train to Tarbes. I thought they would be running fairly frequently.

This area was an important one for the Germans as Pau had a large airfield in the vicinity - also industries, one of which was a factory which made optical instruments and which was then, of course, being run by the Germans. In Tarbes, about twenty-five miles away, there were several factories, including a national arsenal and the car works of Hispano-Suiza. The former was making guns, the latter aero-engines. The Hispano-Suiza works had been hit by saboteurs in August, but the work continued

again after a day or two. The underground cells were very active in
this region, but they were always in great danger as there were so
many Germans about. One very effective cell was working under
British leaders, and several other groups were engaged in
operating the escape routes set up for access over the Pyrénées into
Spain and Portugal.

As I entered the station I saw many soldiers and S.S. officers but
only a few civilians. I felt certain the latter were Gestapo - whatever their clothes they were unmistakable. I walked past them
without appearing to notice them. There was a train standing at
the platform, but the ticket barrier was unmanned; I walked
through to see what the train was doing there, intending to go
back for a ticket if it was due to leave for Tarbes without too long a
delay. There was no one but myself on the platform, and the
stationary train was empty. I realised at once that something
unusual was happening. Further along the line, in the direction
of Tarbes, stood two other trains, blocking the one at the
platform. All movement was at a standstill. I wondered whether
sabotage somewhere on the line had halted them; or perhaps they
were waiting to receive a whole consignment of troops or
prisoners. Whatever the reason, there would be no normal
passenger train leaving for Tarbes for a long time to come, and
meanwhile here was I, a civilian, alone and conspicuous, the very
thing I wished to avoid.

I glanced round nervously. No one had followed me, no official
approached to ask me what I was doing there. This in itself was
suspicious at a time when one could scarcely move a step without
being questioned. I remembered then that as I went on to the
platform I had seen two soldiers walk away from the station. Had
I been recognised? It was possible that there were posters about
with my description. But I had not been arrested or followed.
Perhaps they reckoned on my not being able to leave the station
without being seen and intercepted ...

I had no intention of leaving the station by the way I had
entered. I do not know what was in the minds of the Germans, but
if they meant to trap me here they made a big mistake in not
keeping me under observation, because I knew this station very
well indeed. I knew that towards Tarbes one could get off the
railway line onto a National road. It meant getting along the line
out of sight before making for the road. Luck was with me. I
entered one of the carriages of the train that stood at the platform,
climbed out the other side, and crawled along the line. I entered

and left the second train further along the line, then got into the third train - all were empty of passengers. I left the third train and again crawled until I was out of sight of the station. Then I walked along the line until I could find a convenient spot to get on to the road. I knew that if the Germans failed to find me in the station they would have to search every carriage of the three trains, and it would be some time before they realised I had got clean away. I reached the main road quite easily and hurried along in the direction of Tarbes.

As I walked along the road I heard the sound of a car and looked behind me. A blue-grey Austin was coming towards me, and for a moment I thought I was dreaming, for it looked exactly like my own car. Then I remembered that mine had been sprayed khaki and was now in London. As it approached I looked again and saw that it was being driven by a German officer. It drew alongside me and stopped. I stopped also, and saw to my relief that the officer was not one of the S.S. but a General of the Wehrmacht, most of whom were not Nazis.

He spoke to me in fairly good French and asked me where I was going. This was the first human being I had heard speak for fourteen days, and for a moment I hesitated. Then I told him I was going to visit my aunt who had a villa on the outskirts of Tarbes. He said he was passing through Tarbes and would drive me as far as my aunt's villa. I got into the car and sat next to him. I wondered where he had acquired it. Probably locally - there had been a great number of British living in Pau and the surrounding area before the war. The golf course there was popular and had an English professional who gave lessons. Also the Pau Hunt was run by an American Master of Hounds, and the huntsmen and whips were British. It had a large following among the British and German hunting society.

The General drove on at a leisurely pace, as if he were in no hurry to deliver me at my aunt's house. My friends' house was actually on the Tarbes road and I did not want him to see it and be able to identify it, but there was nothing I could do at the moment. He asked me what I did in life; did I work? I told him that I was a schoolteacher and lived near Pau. I said that my aunt had been ill and as it was impossible to get young domestic staff I intended to ask her to spend some time with me. I wanted him to think I was based near Pau. I was afraid that he might ask more specific questions but instead he began to talk about the war, and especially about the British. He said he had had many British friends before the war; he thought that all wars were terrible and unnecessary.

I said, 'Hitler does not think so!'

He ignored my comment, and continued to talk about the British and how much he liked them. I tried to turn the conversation away from the British, but without success. Why was he harping on about them to me, a Frenchwoman - as far as he knew? I began to have an uneasy feeling that he must suspect me of being a British agent, though there seemed no reason why he should do so. Even if a description of me had been circulated, it would not be as an Englishwoman. 'You know,' he said, 'the Germans and the British have a good deal in common.'

'You seem to like British cars,' I remarked. I hoped he might start to talk about cars; perhaps he would tell me how he came to possess the Austin. He said nothing more for a while, but kept glancing at me and drove more slowly than ever. The feeling that he had somehow seen through my disguise grew stronger every moment, but at the same time I was almost convinced that he was sincere in what he had been saying, that he hated the war and was sympathetic towards the British. I did not want to kill him, but could not risk the safety of myself or my friends. Hoping that he would let me go and save me the decision, I said, 'Thank you for the lift. If you drop me here, I can easily walk on to my aunt's villa.'

'It's no trouble,' he said. 'I'll take you as far as the house.'

The house was almost in sight now; the situation was desperate. I started to get myself into the necessary Karate position. The car was going quite slowly, and my lungs were working well ... I think the General must have known something about Karate himself. He may have felt me stiffen, because quite suddenly he stopped the car, leaned over, opened the door and pushed me out. I was half in and half out of it. I had to let the air out of my lungs, or I would have concussed my nervous system. I got the rest of my body out of the car and stood like an idiot waiting for him to make the next move. I expected him to cover me with his revolver and arrest me, and yet my strongest emotion was relief that I had not got as far as attacking him.

'I hope,' he said politely in very good English, 'that you will find your aunt in better health.' Then he pulled the door to and drove on. I stood and watched the Austin until it disappeared down the road to Tarbes.

I walked slowly on towards the villa, wondering whether I

ought to go inside. Supposing he meant to report to the Gestapo
... once more the decision was taken out of my hands, for my
friends had seen me pushed out of the car, and as soon as it drove
away they ran out of the house and hustled me in. I explained that
I had been about to kill the General, but he had been too quick for
me.

'What a pity you failed,' said my friends. I said nothing, but in
my heart I was ashamed that I, whose life had been saved by a
miracle, had been so close to killing another human being in cold
blood.

It was some time before I could have that bath of my dreams. My
friends had tunnels in their grounds which they had furnished
and stocked with provisions in preparation for an emergency, and
we all remained hidden there for three days. I took very small
portions of food and drink every two hours to enable my stomach
to function properly, and dozed a good deal. When no unwelcome
visitors arrived we came to the conclusion that I had been given a
lift by a German General who was making his own escape. My
Portuguese friends said there were strong rumours that many
Wehrmacht officers had revolted; some had been shot, others were
trying to escape.

We heard later that three German officers of the Wehrmacht
had surrendered themselves to the Swiss Embassy in Lisbon and
that one of them had an Austin car - we never learnt its colour.
Looking back, I wondered whether the General had been putting
out feelers, hoping that I might help him to escape. I fervently
hoped that he was one of those who had succeeded. Surely there
were not many who owned Austins. It was possible that by giving
me a lift and getting me clear away from Pau he had saved my life.
I was more thankful than ever that I had not taken his.

After three days we emerged from our hiding-place and I had
the long-awaited bath. It was worth waiting for. I had all the hot
water and perfume that I had promised myself, and my hostess
provided me with fresh underclothing. No medicine could ever
have achieved this wonderful clean feeling.

I now felt fully recovered. I managed to get in touch with Jules
in Lyon, who was delighted to hear that I had got through safely.
He said there had been a great hue and cry for several days, and he
had seen posters giving a description of me and a fairly good
identikit picture. They had no name for me. They called me the
'Unknown Woman'. How odd, I thought, that I should be known
to my enemies by the same name my pilot Mike had given me.

I told Jules that I would make my way to Limoges, and asked for 'group' help. He said he would make all the arrangements. Then I got in touch with England to report my safety and asked for permission to go north, as I wanted to find out what the heavy vehicles were which I had heard on the National routes near Pau. My Portuguese friends provided me with a full-length coat and a hat and handbag, so that my appearance was changed. I did not use any make-up and I looked quite inconspicuous. I knew that I would have to be very carful now that my description had been circulated, but the thought that my group would be working with me gave me courage. My Tarbes friends had many contacts, and I was able to get transport to Limoges.

I met Jules and Pierre at Limoges and we went to Châteauroux. From here I made contact with one of the brothels in Lyon where I had friends, and they gave me a great deal of information on the movement of Panzer divisions moving from the south to the north.

The Germans were very active in the Lyon area. Many underground cells were tracked down and many arrests were being made. It was obviously very dangerous to move around. Once when I was in Jules' car we passed a poster with the picture of the Unknown Woman and I wanted to have a look at it, but Jules would not stop. Of course he was right. Patrols were out each night where there were fields where a plane might land. I arranged for a pick-up, and that night the brothel girls were very actively engaged in inviting patrols in for drinks. The pick-up was successful, but soon afterwards forty brothel girls were shot as members of Resistance. These girls were true patriots and very courageous.

19

The Jackboot Grows Heavier

I was glad to be back at Tempsford, where I was met by both majors. I did not want to talk in the car going back to London; the traumatic experiences I had been through had caught up with me, and reaction had set in. The Major, who was driving, was very understanding and when we arrived at the flat he made no move to come in, but simply said, 'You'll find a bottle of brandy in the stores. Have a large one and go to bed.' The R.E. major pressed my hand, and they both left.

I was too exhausted even to take a bath. I undressed and washed my face and hands in cold water, then followed the Major's advice - I poured a large brandy, downed it and went to bed, where I went out like a light and knew no more till well on in the morning. I was grateful that the Major did not call too early. By the time he arrived I was dressed and enjoying my first cup of coffee. He gave me a long, hard look and said, 'Well, Jay Bee, I'm glad to see you're back in circulation.'

I felt that I was back, and eager to know the result of my efforts. I asked, 'Was my journey really necessary?'

'You'll never know how necessary!'

'You liked my package, then?'

'It was a very useful package indeed - much more useful alive than dead. But so are you, Jay Bee - you gave us a horrible fright. You should have come back with him.'

I explained what I had been told about the Lysanders, how I feared my added weight would make things risky for the pilot. He nodded, but said, 'It was a greater risk for you, to do as you did.'

He was looking at me as if he still did not quite believe I was there, as large as life if a little thinner than before. He said, 'I am afraid the information we gave you was not quite correct. The man's mother was not a widow. She was dead; it was his father who was living.'

I felt in retrospect the tingling at the nape of the neck that seemed to warn me of unforeseen dangers. No wonder I had felt it outside the hotel at Lyon! My carefully concocted cover story was based on incorrect information; I was known to be a phoney from the station onwards. I put up a hand to smooth my hair as if it was still literally rising from my scalp.

'I am sorry about that, Jay Bee,' said the Major, and I wondered when he had learnt the truth and discovered that he had let me walk into an already baited trap. I said, 'It doesn't make any difference now. I am safe and you've got the information you wanted.' As he was evidently feeling that he owed me something, I dared to ask,' What has become of the man?'

'At the moment, he is indisposed.' The answer was not very illuminating, but I knew it was no use persisting. It was no longer my affair. I never learnt what happened to this man, and I am not sure I wish to know.

I felt that I had gathered a good deal of useful information, but the Major first wanted a detailed account of my adventures. I related the whole story, ending with my long walk to Pau, the miracle that had saved me, my confrontation with the General in the Austin and the final pick-up. He did not interrupt me till I came to the end, then shook his head wonderingly and said, 'You certainly are one of the chosen, Jay Bee. I am sure you will always be guided and guarded.'

When I had reported on the Panzer divisions and everything else I had learnt, I felt very tired again, and he told me to relax completely for a couple of days. He provided me with food and drink and I was able to relax in comfort and digest the recent events that I had lived through. I came to the conclusion that it was no fun being 'one of the chosen'; but that if this meant experiencing a miracle and being given the opportunity of being of real service to my country, then I would not wish it to be otherwise.

I did not go to Storey's Gate after this last assignment. I was told that Churchill was having many discussions at this time and was under great pressure. He would be leaving the country on various missions in early November and we would not see him again until December.

The Major said that there were disturbing reports coming from Paris that many Resistance workers were being arrested, but it would only be possible to obtain a true picture from someone actually in the city. He asked me if I was prepared to go in so that I

could assess the situation myself. Contact was made with Jules in
the Midi, who in turn made contact with Jacques in Paris. It was
arranged that Jules should meet me at Evreux, at the farmhouse
owned by the elderly friends of the Major where I had stayed
previously. A few days later I was on my way to Evreux. Jules met
me at the landing field, not at the farm, which was very
thoughtful of him. He had his car, and as an Inspector of
Railways he could make certain of being in the area without
question.

We were made very welcome at Evreux, but I was shocked at the
change in our friends. They seemed to have aged years in a few
months. They were extremely worried by the continual drain of
labour to the German labour forces inside Germany and into the
French factories under German command. Men and women were
being made to work all hours of the day and night.

The change in our friends was a reflection of the all-round
deterioration in the situation. Resentment was rife among the
French people. A great deal of food was being taken from the area,
and one had to be dishonest about hiding food and falsifying
returns of stock. Our friends on the farm were honest people and
resented having to resort to dishonest practices. Jules laughed
about it and said, 'Treat it as a game - that way it won't hurt so
much.' But I could well understand their feelings. I myself had
been forced to lower my standards and act against my principles.
The only consolation was that I was making a necessary sacrifice,
and that it was only temporary. One had to live for the present and
try not to think of the past or future.

Jules travelled to Paris with me, and his presence gave me a
sense of security. He had a very quick brain and could almost
anticipate what the Germans were thinking. We met Jacques at
one of the Metro stations and Jules left us, saying that he would
meet me there again in three days' time. Jacques was still
concierge at the flats and we walked through the streets to the Ile
St Louis. It was my first visit to Paris since my arrest by the
Gestapo, and I was glad of Jacques' company. He was much
quieter than usual, and I remarked on this. He shrugged
expressively and said, 'To speak at all is dangerous now, and one
has to be careful even of thinking.' He told me that in Paris and its
environs there were over thirty thousand Gestapo. They had taken
over many buildings in the 16th *arrondissement* and a great many
arrests had been made in this area, where members of Resistance
and French S.O.E. had been active. Many of those arrested were

couriers and radio operators, but the most important agent arrested was the 'Indian Princess'. She had been taken to the Avenue Foch, the H.Q. of Gestapo interrogation. He thought that her cell had been betrayed.

I have often wondered why this girl, Noor Inayat Khan, code name Madeleine, was ever sent to Paris as an agent. I had met her there before the war. She used to write radio plays and scripts for the children's programmes and was very well known and popular. She was a rather fey type and very attractive, and once seen would always be remembered. Although she spoke French fluently she had a slight foreign accent and would never be able to disguise herself as a Parisian. Once she had been seen or heard the Germans would undoubtedly check on her. Jacques said that she had left Paris in 1940 with her family. He thought she had made a great mistake in coming back and had been careless about being seen so much in Paris in 1943. It was asking for trouble.

I heard afterwards that she had been betrayed by one of the members of her cell, but I do not know whether this is true or not. Unfortunately, when she was arrested at her flat in Paris the Germans found her receiving and transmitting radio. She had recorded codes and messages in an exercise book. It was a great haul for the Germans. When I heard about this I thought how wise it was of Winston Churchill to choose a woman for his Circle - myself - who could rely entirely on a photographic memory.

We shall never know why Madeleine kept codes, cyphers and messages recorded in a book for anyone to find. The Germans took possession of it and it was known afterwards that they used it to advantage until 'receivers' in England became suspicious and false information was returned. One can however say with conviction that when she was interrogated by the Gestapo she kept silence. She was tortured, starved, stripped of her clothing, and when naked was put into chains. She was kept in solitary confinement for many months and eventually executed in September 1944 at Dachau. Two other women were executed with her; Yolande Beckman (code name Yvonne) a member, like Madeleine of the W.A.A.F., and Elaine Plewman (code name Gaby) who was a member of F.A.N.Y.

When one realises the indignities and the sufferings that Madeleine was subjected to, and the fact that she was of Indian descent, born in Russia, and not a European, one can only have the greatest admiration for a courageous woman. It was not really her fight, but she made it so. We owe so much to these brave women and their endurance.

I got a lot of information from Jacques about the feelings of the people of Paris. The Germans had a great deal of support from some, but amongst the majority there was growing hatred towards the occupation force. Gaullist Resistance cells were forming fast. I understood Jacques' fear of speaking or even thinking. There were so few people one could really trust.

Having learnt a great deal in three days I made arrangements to return to England. I met Jules at the Metro station at the appointed time and he escorted me on the train and then to our rendezvous for the pick-up. The Major was waiting at the flat and he looked worried. I told him of the change in both the Germans and the French. Fear and hatred were growing on both sides. The French grew more careless as they grew more desperate, and Jacques suspected that many of the Resistance people were betraying their comrades because they were being tortured so ruthlessly. The Major agreed when I said I would hesitate to blame them. It required a certain extraordinary type of courage to withstand torture such as the Germans used.

Two days after my return I received a message from my cousin Jo. We had been able to communicate with each other by telephone, but we had never met since she had become my stand-in. This time, however, she had matters which she urgently wanted to discuss with me, and the Major arranged for us to meet. The Prime Minister had left the country on a mission, so we could not consult him. We had to meet very secretly, as we must not be seen together. It was not a happy reunion, as Jo had had a personal tragedy. I explained this to the Major, and said that she might have to leave London. He agreed that she could no longer double for me, and it was arranged that she should give up her work for the M.E.W. and I should take over from her there until the end of December. After that I would retire, on the pretext of illness.

When I returned to the M.E.W. I found that plans for Overlord were almost completed. The actual date of invasion was still to be decided, but S.H.A.E.F. had taken over C.O.S.S.A.C. (Chiefs of Staff Supreme Allied Command); the 21st Army Group was much in evidence. General Eisenhower had chosen his aides with care, and the Americans had supreme command. Eisenhower was a great statesman, in whom one could have confidence; also

Churchill had 'Brookie' at the War Office and 'Monty' in the field, so all seemed to be going well.

Churchill did not return in December as expected. He had caught a chill in that month, became seriously ill and almost died. It was said that his life had been saved by drugs, but personally I believe that it was the arrival of his wife which turned the scales. For some time it was considered too dangerous for her to fly out to him, but finally she insisted and was flown to Marrakesh. A friend who was there told me of the outcome. He was lying unconscious, barely able to breathe, when she came into the room. As soon as she touched his hand his breathing became easier, and from that moment he began to recover. I know it has been said by many people that if he had died during this illness we would still have defeated the Germans; I do not believe this. I believe that a Conditional Surrender would have been arranged. Churchill was always adamant that this time an Unconditional Surrender must be enforced to ensure future peace in Europe, but there were many people who did not agree.

I faded out of the M.E.W. scene at the beginning of January 1944 and Jo left London in February of that year.

The cells in France had been crying out for equipment so that they could help when Liberation came. It was also thought necessary to drop equipment into France to await the Liberation troops; it would save space for the armada which would be liberating France and Europe. Between January and May 1944 over fifty thousand pieces of equipment were dropped in. Many planes were brought down and air-crews were in danger, but the escape routes were open and Resistance ready to help. One of the busiest was the Pat O'Leary Line. Resistance groups were also able to get hold of most of the equipment and hide it from the Germans.

In early February 1944 I returned to Normandy. There was a great deal of activity in the area and rumours were floating around. Apparently General Rommel was seen quite often in the district where he had taken up his command. The Wehrmacht had been in occupation there for a long time and had been fairly easy-going, but when Rommel arrived they were more alert. There were S.S. regiments there as well, and these were much disliked.

Pierre and Antoine were in this district, and they informed me that the underground cells of the Gaullists were joining up with other cells. A new army of Frenchmen was being formed, known as the E.M.F.F.I., Etat-Major des Forces Françaises de l'Interieur. They could not all have uniforms, but it had been arranged for brassards (arm bands) to be worn by those not in uniform. I thought this was asking for trouble. The German Army would respect a uniform, but not an arm band, and I could visualize great carnage. The Gestapo and S.S. would respect nothing, not even a regulation uniform; they were simply killers. General de Gaulle arranged for the arm bands to be worn as soon as Liberation started. His very able General Koenig was responsible for forming the new Army of France.

Pierre told me that he had heard of a priest who was said to travel between Caen and the Pas de Calais. He did not know if he was a real priest or one of the Gestapo in disguise, but it was significant that whenever he appeared in a district there were many arrests of Resistance members. Eventually Jules discovered that he was a Frenchman working for the Gestapo, and determined to get rid of him. In April 1944 the 'priest' was killed by someone in Resistance and his body disappeared.

I was more than ever alarmed at the seeming carelessness of the underground cells. If it increased, the Gestapo hunts would also increase. There were signs already of this happening. Jules kept his eyes open when he was travelling about inspecting railways, and he said that a great number of strangers were arriving in the district, mostly civilians, and he suspected that they were Germans.

On my return I told the Major of my anxiety about the use of the arm bands. He said we could do nothing about it. It was de Gaulle's affair, and the General would certainly not welcome criticism. De Gaulle was in charge of Defence for the Algerian French government and though General Giraud was still the overall representative of France, it was obvious to many that eventually General de Gaulle would be in complete charge. He was ambitious and had the support of the bulk of the French and American officers in Algiers.

I was glad to rest for a couple of days. The Major had stocked the store cupboard with tins of fruit and - surprise of surprises in those days of shortages - a lovely tin of biscuits.

20

Build-up to Liberation

The Major told me I would be going to Paris again. He thought Jacques could give me more accurate information about what was happening than some of the confused accounts that were coming in. I suggested that surely the Bletchley people could help; with their secret method they could pick up and decode Hitler's orders to his generals. The Major said that this was not enough. The Prime Minister wanted on-the-spot information.

Three days later Jules, Pierre and Georges met me near Tours and Jules saw me on to the train for Paris. I had arranged to meet Jacques at Boris and Janine's café on the Avenue de la Grande Arméé, and was given a great welcome by all three. Boris said the place was crawling with Gestapo in and out of uniform. He was disgusted with some of the S.S. soldiers who visited his café - they were Frenchmen.

'I have to give wine to the pigs,' he snorted. 'If I had my way I'd give them poison. But they'll meet their doom some day. We shall not forget.'

The Major had asked me to find out all I could about a 'pilotless plane', parts of which, it was rumoured, were being made in Paris. When I mentioned this to Jacques he said he had heard that the mushroom cellars around Paris were being used to build a special kind of bomb which could fly. I asked him where he had got this information and he told me that several Polish soldiers of the Wehrmacht were on guard there and some of his Maquisards had made friends with them and had drinks with them. One of them had talked about the bomb and about 'launching pads' on the coastlines of Northern France and Belgium, which were forbidden zones. Jacques said he had not taken this talk seriously. A bomb that flew! Could one imagine a more absurd idea. The flying bomb was in fact the V1, commonly known as the doodlebug later by the British people.

To me, on the other hand, this news sounded as though it might be very important. When I questioned him further Jacques said he had noticed that many Germans reputed to be scientists had left Paris - they had either gone to another part of France or returned to Germany. I wondered whether this had a connection with the bomb.

I also learnt from Jacques that the good Wehrmacht officers were being moved and S.S. officers were taking their places. He mentioned a German named Goetz who had the reputation of having a sharper nose for enemy agents than even Sergeant Bleicher. He had a charming manner; he did not threaten but gained people's confidence and then pounced. It was said that he was a friend of Himmler and worked under direct orders from the Gestapo Führer.

When Jacques and I left the café we went to the Ile St Louis flat, where I was going to stay. When I asked him where his friend Marie was, he told me she was on a visit to her parents and he was meeting her the following day at the Gare St Lazare. Would I like to go with him? I said I would, but when we reached the station Jacques was worried by the sight of so many Gestapo at the barriers - far more than usual. Some were in uniform and others appeared to be civilians, but one could easily identify them. Jacques was sure they were on the look-out for someone special, and suggested that we separate, so while he waited near the barrier I walked about looking, I hoped, quite uninterested in whatever was happening. I noticed a man come into the station, and as he approached I recognised him as Yeo-Thomas, whom I had known before the war when he was a director of Molyneux Fashion House.

I had to stop him from walking into a trap. I went towards him, bumped into him, and dropped my handbag. I pretended to be annoyed, and as he stooped to pick up the bag I whispered in English, 'Gestapo at all barriers, get away if you can.' He coolly handed me the bag, raised his hat and left the station. I still pretended to be angry and muttered to myself in French as I brushed my handbag with my handkerchief.

I saw Jacques and Marie coming towards me. They did not stop, but Jacques winked as they walked to the station exit. I followed after a few minutes and we met outside. I hoped the incident of my bump into Yeo-Thomas had not appeared intentional. When no one followed us I felt sure that it had not attracted any undue attention, but I hoped he would leave Paris, for he must be a marked man.

Marie had met some of Jacques' Communist Maquis friends, and she told us that many of them were joining up with the Gaullist groups. Jacques said that his group would still work on their own; he disliked the Gaullists and did not trust them. Marie said there were many more German soldiers about in all areas around Paris. When were the British coming? Four years of occupation was quite long enough and she wanted to see the end of the Germans. It was difficult to explain to people living under this oppression that it was no use our invading until we could be certain of victory.

I left Paris the following day and was surprised to see Jules at the station. He told me he would be on the train but was getting off at the station before Tours, and advised me to do the same. We travelled separately, but when I got off the train as he had advised me he explained that Tours station was under siege by the Gestapo and everyone was being searched. He had arranged a car to take me to friends of his who lived near the rendezvous for the plane; he, Pierre and Georges would see me on to the plane when the pick-up was fixed.

I felt I had been lucky in gathering so much information in the short time I had been in Paris. The Major was especially interested in the talk about the flying bomb. I told him about my meeting with Yeo-Thomas and said I thought he was in great danger and should be brought home. The Major explained that although he had every sympathy with him there was nothing he could do about it. I was in the Secret Circle, while Yeo-Thomas was working more with de Gaulle than with us, as he was with F.S.O.E. (French S.O.E.).

I was very sad about this, though I realised that the matter was out of our hands. Unfortunately my fears were justified. He was arrested a short time later when he was entering a Metro station. The Germans tortured him, and how he survived was a miracle, but he gave them no information. He escaped with others from Buchenwald concentration camp when the Americans were fighting near there, and was able to make contact with them. He played a great part in helping to form, with General Koenig, the new French Army.

On the evening after my return we went to Storey's Gate, where Churchill greeted us with obvious pleasure. I told him how pleased I was that he had recovered from his dangerous illness. He thanked me and went on to say how much my successful capture of the cement expert in the autumn had contributed to the Liberation plans.

'I suppose, sir,' I said modestly, 'that being a freak helped.'

'Freak?' he echoed, mystified, and looked at the Major and then back to me. I mischievously left the explanation to the Major.

'I am afraid, Prime Minister,' he said, 'that Ernie Bevin has been talking to Jay Bee. Your remark about ninety-five per cent brain ...'

I saw by Churchill's expression, half caught out, half amused, that recollection had dawned.

'Let me tell you, sir,' I said, 'that you are quite wrong about the other five per cent. I have as much sex as any woman - given the time and place.'

He burst out laughing, then with a lift of the eyebrows enquired, 'You wouldn't care to tell me what time and what place?'

I had no reply ready. He usually managed to have the last word.

We stayed some time and I learnt that the date of Overlord, the code name for the invasion, would be decided very soon. As we left he said, 'I shall see you some time in May, Jay Bee,' from which I concluded that D-Day was likely to be in late May or early June, and that my next assignment would be directly connected with it. The Major came back to the flat and we talked until the early hours of the morning. What he said confirmed my own ideas about Overlord. He told me to rest for a few days, and I was glad of the chance to relax and see to my personal affairs.

On a fine spring day I walked through Hyde Park and went on to Kensington Gardens. All about me nature was coming back to life, and France seemed a long way off. I could not help wondering how the people of London would react under Occupation. I thought of our East Enders. I could not imagine them yielding. I think there would have been a great blood bath. The East Enders of London love their country and they love their monarchy; they love the pageantry of London, and they do not change. Many people have tried to change them, but fundamentally they remain the same.

A week later the Major came to the flat and gave me the news that the date of D-Day had been decided, and I would know it soon. He wanted me to return to Normandy, contact my best men, and make a visit to an address near Falaise which I was to memorise. If we could get to this address and make ourselves known to the occupants it would be of value later on. I had a week in which to make the contact.

My best men were Jules, Pierre, Antoine and François, and

these four met me at the rendezvous as arranged. I was to be picked up in seven days' time at the same place for my return to England. I told the men what we were to do and they said that there were increased troop movements in the area. Our biggest fear was the Militia. The men had never before seen so many Militia and Gestapo in this district and we would have to be very wary. Jules said that General de Gaulle was broadcasting from Algiers to the people of France and raising their hopes, and the people were not cautious enough. It was not for me to criticise de Gaulle's policy. I said that he was in charge of the Algiers government and would do what he thought was best, but they could be sure the British would not return to France unless they were certain of success.

We reached Falaise without any trouble; Jules, Antoine and François had the love birds on their papers and Pierre had papers for post and telegraph, which made things comparatively easy for us. We made contact with the people at the address I had been given. They were friends of the Major, the wife French, the husband Portuguese, and they were expecting us. I told them I might be in touch with them later with news for the Major, and they said I would be welcome at any time, and my men also. They warned us that many S.S. soldiers were in billets in the area, and some in camps.

They had a beautiful house and garden. I could not help thinking of the forthcoming Liberation and the inevitable destruction that would follow, and wondered whether this property would survive; so much beauty was being destroyed. I tried to console myself with the thought that while some men destroy others preserve; the pendulum swings both ways, and one day soon it would surely swing back in the right direction.

After leaving Falaise I had three days to spare and I decided to visit Caen. I told the men I was going to a café there, and they said they would have a look round and meet me later.

The café was nearly empty and I ordered coffee - such as it was - and a brandy. There was a German officer, Wehrmacht by his cap, sitting at a nearby table. He smiled at me, so I smiled back. He came over to my table and asked if he could join me; I nodded and he sat down. He was wearing a trench mac which he removed, and I saw that he was a senior officer. He asked me if I was married, and had I a home in Caen? 'No,' I replied, 'I am not married. I relieve at various schools when there is a shortage of teachers.'

He hesitated for a moment and then said, 'How strange. I was once a schoolteacher myself. It was a long time ago.' His French was good, and I had the feeling I knew him; then I suddenly recognised him as Le Bosche, the Military Governor of the district, the one who lived at Bayeux. He continued, 'War is a very terrible affair. I long to be home with my wife and family. Do you think the British will ever return to fight in France?'

'I don't know,' I replied. 'We have been waiting four years for them, so it does not seem likely. We have become used to you and your soldiers.'

'Yes,' he said, 'I must admit you people have behaved very well and my task here has been an easy one. But if the British do come back I shall not fight them. I shall try to get home. I am tired of war.'

Before I could make any comment he stood up, saluted me, and left. I was impressed by his personality and of course very interested in his views. He was a charming German, and on D-Day I think he must have carried out his decision, because the British were in Bayeux the day after invasion. I hope he arrived home safely to his family.

My men had seen me talking to him and had been worried about me. I told them I had recognised him so had been very careful. Jules said, 'He is a good Boche, that one.' Pierre frowned and said, 'All Germans are bad. Some are worse than others, but there are no good Germans.'

I told him there were good and bad in every nation, but he shook his head doubtingly. Pierre was still young enough to see the world in black and white; he could not distinguish the many shades of grey.

I stayed with friends of Jules until I was ready to be picked up, and was seen off by my four companions.

The Major told me about the meeting of the War Cabinet, when General Eisenhower had announced his plans for the landings. General de Gaulle was at the meeting at which Eisenhower announced that he would make a proclamation to the people of France, and false money would be dropped to confuse the Germans. De Gaulle was angry and thought that it should be he who made the proclamation, but Churchill reminded him that it was an Allied operation and General Eisenhower was Supreme Commander.

Eisenhower went on to say that all the representatives of German occupied countries would be given the opportunity to broadcast to their people over the B.B.C. on D-Day, and he named them in order. He named France last and de Gaulle blew his top, left the meeting in disgust and returned to Algiers. A few days later the date was announced - but de Gaulle did not attend and therefore did not know the date. It was decided after consultation with the long range weather men that it should be between the dates of June 1st and June 10th.

The cells in France were told to listen to the B.B.C. nine o'clock news on dates during May; when, after the news, they heard a line read in French from the poem *The Song of Autumn* by Verlaine, they would know that the Invasion was imminent. The line would be:

'Les sanglots longs des violons de l'automne'

When they heard the second line, invasion would be within twelve hours. This line was:

'Blessent mon coeur d'une longueur monotone'

General Eisenhower had not mentioned which plan would be used for the Resistance and the people of France on invasion. The original British plan under C.O.S.S.A.C. was to call for a graduated uprising of the people as many provinces would have no means of defence. The Americans, under S.H.A.E.F., favoured a general uprising.

Plans for Liberation had been very well thought out. One had to bear in mind that there were many Communist groups who might try to take over during the invasion. This had been foreseen and men had been trained to be dropped in to take over the groups and cells of Resistance. The 'Jed Boys' (Jedburgh Teams) were composed of one American, one French, and one British officer, plus a radio operator. These men would be in uniform. Teams of S.A.S. would be in the advance guard in groups of ten to twelve men. These were also a secret force, trained to combat, and would be behind enemy lines very quickly. With them would be one hundred and fifty Frenchmen who had trained with them. The Frenchmen wanted to be the first on French soil after having been in Britain for four years. One could understand their feelings.

The S.A.S. would make contact with Resistance. On arrival, passwords were to be 'I am looking for a four-leaved clover' and 'the tomatoes must be picked'. The Resistance groups would await orders from Britain, to be relayed by radio, to put in action the colour plans. The Green Plan was to disrupt railways and marshalling yards, the Blue Plan to disrupt the post and telegraph services. The Tortoise Plan dealt with roads and bridges.

The planning for the Liberation of Europe had taken several years. Churchill had repeatedly said, 'We dare not lose the war'. I felt that the time had been chosen correctly. One knew that there would be many deaths, but it had to be. Thousands must die so that millions would survive.

21

The Headmistress

It was obvious to everyone living in France in 1944 that the Vichy government existed in name only. The Germans were in control of the whole country. They boasted of their impregnable Atlantic Wall, but it was no secret to us. We knew all about it, and the many gaps in it. There may have been a reason for these gaps, but when Rommel took over command he was clearly worried, and he cement and steel barriers put up on the edge of the beaches to make it difficult for an invading force. The beaches were heavily mined, but the Germans underestimated the Allies, particularly the British. We are islanders, and as such are familiar with coastlines and always study them carefully and know their weaknesses.

The Germans never realised how many of their top secrets we had penetrated. Our own, on the other hand, were well kept: the Bailey Bridges, the Mulberry Harbours, the Pluto Line, the Ultra System. Pluto (pipe-line under the ocean) was a great success and began to pump petrol into France after June 10th, 1944.

At the beginning of May the Major came to the flat to discuss, as he said, my last assignment before Operation Overlord was launched. He stayed all day as there was so much to plan, and we only stopped for a short lunch interval.

I was to go to Caen where, on May 20th, I would be taking up a position as Headmistress of a residential school with forty children who were victims of tuberculosis. It was a private concern and nothing to do with the French Education Authorities. The present Headmistress was supposedly giving up the post because of ill health; in point of fact she was a member of an independent cell, and was going so that I could take her place. Apparently the Major knew her, and had made this arrangement. The staff would not know that I was anything but their new Headmistress. I was not to trust them because, although not friendly with the Germans, they had accepted them.

My task would be to find out before June 5th - D-Day, where Rommel was deploying his tanks. This information had to be obtained if possible by June 3rd, the latest time being June 4th. It was to be taken to our friends at Falaise, who would then get it to the Major. He warned me that it was a dangerous assignment and I might not be able to leave the school myself, so I must be prepared to use my men. One of them would visit the school each day so that if I had any information he could bring it out. I suggested that Pierre was the ideal choice; once, when he was stopped by a Gestapo officer, I had seen him drop to the ground pretending that he was having an epileptic fit, even frothing at the mouth. I never discovered how he did this - it looked absolutely genuine.

I asked the Major what would happen to the children on June 5th. He said that, with the help of my men, arrangements could be made for them to be collected on June 2nd. The staff would be told they were to visit a special hospital, but in reality they would be taken south to safety. The Falaise friends would arrange the transport vehicles.

I knew that our clever Bletchley people had successfully given the Germans the impression that invasion by the Allies would be in the Pas de Calais area. Hitler obviously believed this - the Ultra System was capable of picking up and decoding his orders to his generals. It was clear that he was in charge of all defence and his generals had to carry out his orders.

Both Churchill and Monty were of the opinion that there would be some generals who would not obey Hitler, but would do what they thought best. Rommel was a professional soldier and it was obvious that he had little faith in Hitler at this time. The first attempt on Hitler's life in the autumn of 1943 was a failure, but it was rumoured that Rommel was very dissatisfied with events. Fortunately for him, Hitler still seemed to think that he was his best general.

Rommel would fight the Allies in whatever way he himself thought best. He and Monty were both brilliant generals, but Monty had certain advantages. He was fortunate in having some extremely able generals working with him, as well as the Americans and Canadians and other Allies. I do not think that, as Hitler was giving the orders, Rommel had many advantages other than well disciplined men. He also had the disadvantage of underground Resistance working against him. The more one thinks about this man, the more admiration one has for him. His

family have reason to be proud of him. I have often wished I had
known him.

Three days after my briefing with the Major we visited Storey's
Gate. Churchill was looking much fitter and I could see that he
was in good spirits. He asked me if I fully understood my
assignment and the importance of any information I could get
before D-Day. 'Of course,' he said, 'we can only outline the plan,
Jay Bee. You will have to use your initiative. Is there anything you
are vague about?'

I told him that as I was to take up the position of Headmistress
on May 20th, I should like two days in which to look around Caen
with my men, to brief them. I thought it would be best to go in on
the 17th or 18th. He said, 'It will be arranged.' It occurred to me
that he would have given a lot to go on such an assignment
himself instead of being stuck here at home.

He smiled at me and said, 'I know you will do your best, Jay
Bee. I look forward to your return - in June, I hope.'

'It's a date, sir,' I replied. But I had a strange feeling that
nothing was real any more - this familiar room, myself,
Churchill - would I ever see him again? Would I ever see London
again?

The Major returned to the flat with me, as there was still a great
deal to be planned. He explained that I might not be able to get
back as usual after D-Day if I could not leave before the 5th - not
by Lysander, in any case. He suggested that I could go south and
get in touch with our Portuguese friends, who would arrange
something. I told him not to worry. I had my men and their
friends, as well as the friends in Tarbes; I would manage
somehow. He said I would need plenty of money, but I told him I
did not want to carry much. I had left money with Jacques in Paris
and the men were holding some for me. There was also the
solicitor in the south who had money of mine. The one thing I
was concerned about was luggage; I would need to take more for
this journey. He told me to see to it. He would contact Jules and
arrange the rendezvous, and I would leave on May 17th. He
intended to be in touch daily until May 16th.

He sounded sad. I said, 'I wonder, Major, if we will ever meet
under normal conditions when all this is over. Do you think we
might?'

'I should like it, Jay Bee, but circumstances may prevent it. I
shall certainly never forget working with you. You have worked

like a man, yet remained very much a woman. You are an enigma!'

'I resent that last word!' I protested. 'First I am a freak, then an enigma!'

'Freak was your own word, Jay Bee, don't father it on me! As to enigma - ' he paused, then as once before said, 'It was meant as a compliment.'

We laughed, and were both glad to get back into a lighter key.

In the days that followed I put my personal affairs in order. I wrote a letter to my father to be held by his solicitors if I did not return after hostilities had ceased. Then I arranged for my personal jewellery to be given to the Red Cross for sale - I had already given my silver and other valuables. What are possessions, after all? Most of the time they are just a responsibility.

I was still haunted by the feeling of unreality. Perhaps it was the reaction of former missions; perhaps it was because it was so close to the Liberation of Europe, to which we had looked forward for so long that it was difficult to believe in it. The planning that had gone into Overlord was tremendous. I thought of all the people involved - the M.E.W., the 'Baker Street Boys', the 'Bletchley boys and girls', the S.O.E., the Maquis, the men and women of all the occupied countries. I thought of the people of Brittany, of the Armée Secrète of France which would soon be joined by E.M.F.F.I. Etat-Major des Forces Françaises de l'Intérieur). This force was formed from the existing F.F.I. (Forces Françaises de l'Intérieur) plus many independent cells, plus most of the deserters from the labour force of Frenchmen who were in hiding, waiting for the call to arms. It was reported that over a hundred thousand men and women escaped from the labour force. Many others who were working in German controlled factories managed to sabotage production.

I thought of the Young Partisans of all the countries defying the Germans, men of twenty-one years of age leading them and living in hiding for months on end, and of the British men and women leading groups of saboteurs. I thought too of the fine British and American officers and civilians I had met at the Ministry of Economic Warfare; that hive of brains was something which ought to continue to exist after the war - pooling the intelligence of the people to benefit the people.

I knew the plans for the beaches, Omaha and Utah for the Americans, Juno, Sword and Gold for the British, Canadians and Allies. General Eisenhower had his plans well laid. And I was glad that Monty was in the field. He was well aware that he must lose men, but he did not throw them into battle needlessly, which could not always be said of some others.

At 10.30 p.m. on May 16th the Major escorted me to Tempsford, where we had what I always called the 'famous last meal' - eggs and bacon. We did not talk. Later we were joined by the R.E. major. He said, 'I could not miss saying goodbye.'

'I am coming back, you know,' I told him.

'Of course you are, Jay Bee. What I ought to have said is, "I have come to wish you luck and success".'

Shortly afterwards the plane was ready, and the pilot greeted me with, 'Aren't you cutting things rather fine, Unknown Woman? This surely is a bad time to be going in. France is swarming with Germans.'

We stopped somewhere in England and took on more fuel. Mike said, 'It's going to be risky. I'll glide in at the rendezvous - no landing this time. Drop the suitcase out and then follow it. I'll make it between five and three feet. O.K.? I hope you make it. I've enjoyed our trips, it has been fun.'

'Hardly fun,' I said. 'I have another name for it! Still, I'm delighted to have been flown by such a good pilot. I hope you get through the rest of the war safely. I think all you airmen are fine people - you're a race apart.'

He gave me his usual rather impudent grin, then said, 'Complete silence now. All the best, old girl!'

I put out my tongue at him and he gave the victory sign. We saw the signals and he shut the engine off and began to glide down. He picked up wind direction as we neared the ground, then came the curt order, 'Now!' Out went the suitcase and I followed. I looked up and saw his face for a moment. He blew a kiss, the engine roared and he was gone.

I heard afterwards that he was shot down and killed on the way back to England. I am glad I did not know of his death until after Victory in Europe. He was one of the few who did so much.

My men arrived very quickly from hiding and we hurried away. Jules said we were going to stay with friends of his. They would not ask questions.

One could sense that the atmosphere was charged with hatred and desperation. The Germans, by using the Militia to help them - French against French - and by taking most of the young people for labour in German factories, had roused the people to resist where there had been little resistance before. Many

underground radio operators at this time were on the run or had
been arrested. The German detector equipment was very efficient
and many men and women radio operators had been sent to
concentration camps to be shot or sent to the gas chambers. After
four years under the Nazis the men and women of France, who
had lived humble and quiet lives, were so stirred by grief and
anger that they ignored their natural instinct to stay out of
trouble. Heroism was no longer a vague ideal; it was a passionate
reality. In the weeks before D-Day thousands of people were
tortured. They lived in agony and died shouting 'Vive la France!'

Human emotions are, and always have been, unpredictable.
The Germans had yet to learn just how much the French people
valued freedom.

General de Gaulle spoke to the French nation from Algiers. I
was glad that he had left the April meeting when the date for
Overlord was decided; he did not know the actual date of invasion,
and I feel sure that, had he known, he would have told some of the
F.F.I. The Germans listened in to radio all the time, and the secret
would inevitably have leaked through to them.

I made plans with my four men. I told them about the school
and said that I had arranged for the children to be collected on
June 2nd. A German army lorry was to be used. It was hidden at
the time, but I told them where it was and where they were to take
the children. I thought Antoine could be the driver and Jules the
attendant. They would collect false papers, signed by the Sub-
Prefect, from our friends in Falaise. If they were challenged it
would be up to them to get themselves out of trouble. They had
plenty of time before June 2nd to make their plans. I told them I
would try to take a walk between 4.30 and 5 p.m. each day, and
would go to a café we all knew.

I arranged for Pierre to call at the school every day at about three
o'clock in the afternoon. He was to act as though he was simple.
Pierre found this idea very amusing and looked forward to
playing the part.

Jules' friends were very nice people and did all they could for us
in the way of food and beds. They lived outside Caen towards the
coast. Despite the many Germans and Militia about we managed
to avoid attention. We had all become very experienced at
avoiding Germans. On May 19th we went over our plans again in
detail. The men were to watch for Panzer divisions, and let me
know if they should see anything unusual. The house in Falaise
was to be used in any emergency.

On May 19th I left for the school. It was a large private house not far from the Abbaye aux Hommes. I was greeted by the deputy headmistress, who introduced me to the rest of the staff. They were not very young, and seemed lethargic; there were six of them, plus the deputy and myself. There was an elderly gardener and the domestic staff were also old. I told them I did not intend to change anything as I would, I hoped, only be with them for a short time until their own headmistress was well enough to return.

I said that I understood the children were to visit a hospital in June. They seemed to know, and I imagined the former headmistress had been told of this plan by the Major. I asked if the school was ever visited by the Germans. They said all large institutions and buildings had been checked and interest had been shown in this particular school as the Germans needed billets for their soldiers and officers. General Rommel had been visiting Caen quite a lot in the past months. I appeared not to be very interested in the Germans.

I found my quarters quite good – bedroom, bathroom and sitting room. I listened in to the B.B.C. each night and also picked up many talks from Algiers. I kept my radio and receiving and transmitting set under the bed covered with spare blankets. I said that I considered the domestic staff insufficient in number – which was true – and that I would therefore keep my own rooms tidy. The staff were much impressed.

I found the children quite interesting. They were from Brittany and I was pleased that I could help children from this very fine province. Many of their parents were also suffering from tuberculosis, or recovering from it, and had been moved to this area with their children and were living in or near Caen, where those who were fit for work were employed in factories. Those who were unfit were being treated by the same doctor who attended the children at the school.

I managed to take a walk each afternoon and Pierre visited the school daily as arranged. He had a jerky, gangling walk and wore a permanently foolish grin. I told the staff he was quite harmless and would be useful doing errands for us, and they accepted him without question.

The men reported many Waffen S.S. troops arriving, and I also saw them for myself. There were many Wehrmacht too, but we did not see any Panzer divisions. We had to be very careful when we met outside. We did not want to draw attention to ourselves. The curfew was suddenly brought forward and this meant that one could not be out after a set time unless one had papers with the Gestapo stamp. I managed to get through each day quite successfully with the teaching staff, but the days were passing and I still had little or no information.

On May 28th about a dozen Panzers arrived at the school. Two Panzer officers came in and asked to see the Headmistress. They told me that I must vacate the premises. The children and staff were to be out within twenty-four hours. These men were not Waffen S.S., they were Himmler men, the killers. I had seen the signet ring each officer wore and the dagger in the buckle of the belt. I was very much on my guard. I said it would not be possible to move the school out at such short notice. The children were visiting a hospital on June 2nd or 3rd. Could we not stay until then?

'We have already told you what you must do,' said one of the officers, and I knew that I could not risk an argument. I called the staff and broke the news. We had to be out by midday on the following day. They seemed stunned. I could not blame them, as I had no knowledge of what they might have suffered in the past.

I waited for Pierre to arrive, but he did not come. I decided to risk trying to telephone Jules from the telephone in my sitting room. I asked the staff to pack the children's clothes and their own, and I would try to get transport. I had the telephone number of Jules' friend at the café. I got a message through to him and then I cut off very quickly as I heard a click; I was sure the phone in the office was being lifted.

I immediately left my room and joined the staff. Nothing happened, and I felt confident that the phone had not been lifted until I had finished speaking. I told the staff I would attend to food being packed during the night.

At 10.30 p.m. we heard the sound of tanks, and when we looked out we saw that the Panzers were leaving. I went into the office to see if the two officers were still there. They had left also, and there was nothing in the room belonging to them. I concluded that they had received orders to leave, and was thankful that they had gone. I told the staff to go to bed, and we would talk things over in the morning. Then I rang Jules' friend and told him what had happened, and he said he would get the message to Jules.

I went to bed praying that I would be able to deal with whatever events the next day had in store.

22

Waiting for the Violins

Next morning, May 29th, I left the school at ten o'clock and joined Jules and Pierre, who were waiting nearby. It had worried them when the Germans arrived and then departed. Pierre had been turned back when he tried to reach the school. They said that Germans seemed to be arriving in Caen from all directions. Some had already moved north, but a great number remained in the town. They had not seen many Panzers other than those which had come to the school.

Jules told me that the Germans had found the hidden lorry with which we had hoped to remove the children to safety. This was sad news, but he told me not to worry. He could get two German trucks from the railway where he knew there were several parked; being an Inspector he could walk about the station without arousing suspicion. He said he might have to dispose of two truck drivers, but this was no problem. I reminded him that he would have to have papers to show why he was using the trucks, but he assured me that this would not be difficult. He even had some German uniforms hidden away.

I told Pierre that he must try to visit the school each day, and he promised that he would; he would find a reason to deliver something, which would make his visit look more genuine if the Germans should try to turn him away.

When I returned to the school I told the staff that the children would leave on June 2nd or 3rd as planned. I said that I had arranged transport, but I did not go into details. On the evening of May 31st the Panzers returned with more officers; there were also two detector vans, which looked ominous. They sent for me, and the senior officer asked me why I was still there when I had been told to leave with the children. I said that, as he had left with his men and Panzers, I had concluded that he had changed his plans and did not now want the school premises. I reminded him that he had not told me he was leaving. He said that the children and staff must go, but that I must remain.

I asked, 'Does this mean that I am a prisoner or a hostage?'

'It does not mean either,' he replied stiffly. 'You must remain here in case we need information. I shall take over your office and the staff room. If you wish you may use the small room opposite the staff room.'

He was a good-looking man, very young, I thought not more than twenty-one, and in spite of his stern manner I felt that he was unsure of himself. All the officers were young.

He asked me where my bedroom was, and whether I had other rooms. I told him my rooms were on the top floor. He said that I could keep them but that he wished to inspect them - now. He followed me upstairs and was joined by two other officers. I tried to appear calm, but I was thinking, 'If they look under the bed...' Luckily they did not inspect very thoroughly, and my receiving and transmitting set went undetected. The telephone in my sitting room was covered by an ornamental doll, and I did not think they had spotted that either.

I returned with them to the office. Two other officers had arrived, and I saw that all were Himmler S.S. I realised that it would not be safe for Jules to bring the stolen trucks to the school; I must try to find some other way of transporting the children.

I asked the senior officer if I could send a message to the children's parents to tell them they were being transferred to a hospital. He immediately refused, so I asked if it would be possible for him to let us have transport lorries, or even buses; we would need only two. He asked who would drive the vehicles and I said that members of the staff could drive. We would need passes as well, if this could be arranged. He stared at me for a time before answering and then said, 'You are asking for two buses or lorries, and passes?' He sounded incredulous, but at last said, 'I will think about it.'

I returned to tell the staff, and when they heard what I had asked for they thought I was crazy - they were quite sure the Germans would never agree. It was far more likely that we would all be taken to a camp or shot. I assured them that this would not happen; the Germans had shown no sign of aggressiveness, and I was the only one who had to stay behind. I was not frightened, and they had no reason to fear for themselves. I asked them to be on duty earlier than usual next day, and we retired for the night.

When I came downstairs the next morning the staff were

already about, dealing with the children and telling them to hurry up. I advised them to keep the children upstairs, which meant that they would not be able to go outside. They could keep the schoolroom windows open and let the children get some exercise there.

It was the first day of June, 1944. In five days' time the Allies would be in France. The thought cheered me immensely, and I wished it was possible to tell my men, but I knew it could not be.

I went down to the room which had been allocated to me as an office and found that all the German officers were outside in the grounds. I thought I might take this opportunity of using the telephone to get in touch with Jules. I went upstairs to use my phone in the sitting room; from here I could see the officers through the window, and I took the risk. I managed to get in touch with Jules himself - he was at the *estaminet* with friends. I told him not to use the trucks or come to the school; I believed we would be given the transport I had asked for, and if so he and Antoine were to meet the vehicles carrying the children and take over. I would instruct the staff. Jules said he would arrange for some of his men to watch the school. They would pretend to be workmen.

The officers were still in the school grounds, but I saw that they were returning so I went downstairs again. One of them came over to me and asked me to follow him into the office, which they had taken over. I noticed that a map had been put up on the wall. The officer told me that two vehicles would arrive the following day to remove the children and staff, and passes would be provided for two drivers. I felt triumphant. I thanked the officers for their great kindness and asked if they would like some coffee. 'Is it real coffee?' asked one. I told them it was, and they wanted to know where I had obtained it. 'On the Black Market,' I said. 'You can buy almost anything if you have the money.' They asked if one could get cheese and wine. Wine was easy, I said, cheese not so easy. I told them we had some wine, and asked if they would like some - they were welcome to it. They said they would like it very much and would send a soldier for it. I said one of my staff would gladly bring it; it would be left outside the room for them. I would make the coffee myself and bring it to them.

The senior officer thanked me, and at the same time I saw an officer was pinning another map to the wall. He had a box of marking flags in front of him and I guessed that he was going to mark the maps. This was a lucky break; it might be the very information I needed. I must somehow contrive to stay in the office long enough to 'photograph' the maps in my mind.

I left the office and joined the staff, and arranged for one of them to take some wine along for the Germans. When I told them that I had managed to get transport for the next day they were amazed and delighted. Two of them would have to drive, but this proved no problem as several of them had driven cars for some years. I told them that they would be met by friends of mine when they reached Alençon. I did not tell them that they would meet their former Headmistress there, who would then take over proceedings.

I left the staff to discuss everything among themselves and went to make the coffee for the Germans. When it was ready I took it along to the office and explained to the senior officer that the coffee had taken me longer than usual to make because we kept it hidden, as there was such a shortage. I took cups and saucers from the cupboard and poured out the coffee for them. The maps had now been marked with flags and now I had to stay as long as possible in order to study them. The Germans were drinking their coffee with great satisfaction; it was obvious that they had not had any for some time.

I felt that the mood of the officers had mellowed with the coffee and decided to ask once more if I might let the children's parents know of their removal. I begged the senior officer to change his mind and let me warn the parents, since I myself was not allowed to leave the school. I said I had mentioned before that I had a messenger who came in daily, usually during the afternoon, to take messages for us. He was a great help. The officer asked what age he was, and when I told him about twenty-four he immediately became suspicious and demanded, 'Why is he not in a labour camp?'

I said, 'He suffers from fits, and is considered half-witted.'

'How can a half-wit be trusted to take messages?'

I said the messages were written ones, and he took them to the doctor who attended the children and their parents. He thought for a moment and then said, 'We will let them know.'

This did not suit my purpose at all. I said quickly, 'They might be alarmed and think you are British. Your uniforms are different from those we have been used to seeing.'

He said, 'Don't you like the British here?'

I shrugged. 'We have been waiting for them for four years. Now we have grown used to your people.'

One of the other officers stepped forward and said, 'That is true.

There has been very little trouble in this district.'

The senior officer thought for a moment and then said, 'You have my permission to use your messenger.'

Soon after this the officers sent for me to go to the office. They asked me if I had noticed any French soldiers in uniform in the area. I laughed and said the last French soldier I had seen in uniform was in 1940. They went on to ask if I knew anything about a secret army. I said I knew nothing like that - we teachers were not interested in anything pertaining to military affairs. One of the French-speaking officers continued to talk to me, but I was not really listening. I had not admitted to understanding German, and I was listening to the conversation of the others. I heard one of them say that General Rommel was inspecting defences and would be in Paris by June 6th, and then he was going to Germany to see his family. I was delighted to hear this, as it meant Rommel did not believe the Allies would be invading yet.

I managed to get a good look at the maps again. More flags had been placed, but of a different colour. I think this meant different divisions - infantry possibly - anyhow I intended to explain it on my map, which I hoped to give to Pierre when he came again. I left the officers, who were extremely polite. I had already been told that I would occupy the top of the house alone after the staff and children had left, and that I would be quite safe. I wondered why I was being held in the house, but was consoled by the thought that it was not for long. Only a few more days ...

I went to my bedroom before 9 p.m. as I wanted to listen to the B.B.C. news on my radio if possible. I knew that the second line of the poem was to be read on June 4th, but the first line had not yet been heard. I managed to get the news, and after the news came the first line of the poem:

'Les sanglots longs des violons de l'automne'
The slow sobbing of the violins in the Autumn.

I wondered if the announcer knew how important those words were. All over France the various leaders of the cells would be listening and their spirits would rise. It would be only a short time now before they could fight in the open.

It struck me suddenly how incongruous it was that the haunting, sensuous music of Verlaine's lines should be the signal for the clashing discords of battle.

I hoped that the original C.O.S.S.A.C. plan for a graduated

uprising of the Resistance would be put into action. The S.H.A.E.F. plan for a general uprising would mean a great many deaths, as it had not been possible to drop arms to all the Resistance. Some would have only knives and the hand-made plastic bombs they had been using over the last few years.

I did not feel tired, and I took out of hiding the map that I had already sketched, and added to it the other flags I had seen. I also wrote a note on the back of it to say that Rommel was on leave and was supposed to be in Paris on June 6th, after which he was going to Germany. This would be important news. I hoped that Pierre would be able to visit me on the following day to collect the map and the note.

I did not sleep well, and was glad to be up and about early. The staff were also up early and all was ready for the move. They were distressed that I was not leaving with them, but I convinced them that I had my own plans and all would be well. We explained to the children that they would be leaving the school and would join their parents and friends quite soon. I did not know the final destination of the children - the former Headmistress had made the plans with the help of the Major. I hoped that Jules and Antoine would be able to return to the Caen area after passing the children over to the people concerned.

The German officers did not bother us and the luggage was taken down to await the transport, which arrived at 11.15 a.m. We were surprised and delighted to find that it consisted of two French passenger coaches. There was plenty of room for the children, staff and luggage. The domestic staff were going too. The children were in high spirits as they boarded the buses. The senior officer came out to see the exchange of drivers. The staff who were to drive were given their passes, and one of the drivers who had brought the buses - they were Frenchmen, not Germans - whispered, 'Good luck from the Mayor!'

The Mayor of Caen and his wife were working under the Vichy government, but they helped the Resistance a great deal whenever possible, without the population knowing it. After Liberation, General de Gaulle replaced the Mayor with a man of his own choice, as he believed he had collaborated with the Germans. This was not the case. After the war some members of the Resistance wrote letters of thanks for the help the Mayor had given them.

23

Overlord

After the children and staff had left I went to look round the empty rooms. I was automatically straightening some books on a shelf when I saw that the young senior officer had followed me in. He picked up one of the books and glanced at it. It was about the works of Voltaire. He asked me if I liked Voltaire and I said I did; he was very profound.

'Of course,' said the officer, 'he was German. The French adopted him, as other countries adopted great German writers.'

I stared at him in amazement. He was perfectly serious.

'I know that Voltaire had a great liking for German women,' I managed to say (this at least was true) 'but I always thought he was French.'

'Oh no,' he said, 'I have read all his works and admire them. He is definitely German. The English claim Shakespeare, but he was also a German. When the Führer is in control in Europe he will put the matter right.'

I could only nod; words failed me. I knew that Hitler had ordered many of the classics to be burnt - books, records, music, especially works by Jewish authors and composers - but I had no idea that he had taken such a hold over education. I wanted to laugh at this earnest young man and tell him what a fool he was, but after all, he was just another victim of Nazi propaganda.

'This has been a very pleasant conversation,' he remarked. 'I hope we may talk again.' I smiled approval. I still did not trust myself to speak, but was grateful to Voltaire for continuing the good work which the Black Market coffee had begun; one could now almost have called our relationship friendly.

I followed him downstairs and he asked if I had any more coffee. I told him that I would let him have most of what was left, and also the wine. The staff room had facilities for making the coffee. He thanked me, and then I asked him if he would mind my using my radio. He asked me what I listened to, and I told him any station transmitting music; that was all I was interested in. He gave his permission and I was relieved, because I might need to get a message out on my transmission set.

I stayed in the small office downstairs, and waited for Pierre to arrive. He did not come, and I became very worried and restless. Early in the evening I went to my room on the top floor. I dared not use the telephone as I knew the officers were working downstairs; I could hear them moving about in the rooms below.

I retired to bed, but woke very early and went downstairs to the kitchen. There were several German soldiers there and they stood to attention when I entered, so I smiled and nodded to them. One of them offered me a cup of coffee, but I pointed to a tin I was carrying to let them know I was going to make my own. As I made the coffee they were sniffing the aroma, and I realised that theirs was not real coffee. I made more than I needed, poured some into a jug and handed it to them. Their appreciation was pathetic and I wondered what sort of stuff they had been drinking. I poured the rest of the coffee into another jug and left it for them. I also left the coffee grounds; I was sure they would use them. I had not eaten anything since the children left, so I helped myself to two home-made rolls which had been left behind when we packed the food for their journey.

I waited in my office for Pierre, and wondered how I could possibly smuggle out my map if he did not come. The Germans had not inquired whether I had sent the message to the parents. If I had been in the senior officer's shoes, I would have suggested phoning the doctor about the children's movements and letting him inform the parents. Were the Germans such machines that this simple way of communication had not occurred to them? Or were they more intelligent than appeared, and had I fallen into a trap? I hoped and prayed that I had not underestimated them.

It was three o'clock in the afternoon when Pierre finally arrived, but he was not alone. He was followed into the room by two senior Gestapo officers; one had a half-circle of flowers around the gold leaf on his uniform. Before any of us had time to speak Pierre staggered and fell to the ground writhing about and frothing at the mouth.

'Who is he?' demanded one of the Gestapo officers. 'What is the matter with him?'

'He does odd jobs and runs errands.' I said. 'He suffers from fits, but they don't last long. I've seen him like this before.'

'Get rid of him!' said the Gestapo officer disgustedly. 'Where are the officers in charge here?' He spoke excellent French.

I pointed to the door of the staff room opposite. 'Through there.'

They both went out. I bent over Pierre and whispered, 'Wait a few moments and then get up'. I told him hurriedly that I was giving him a paper and he must get it to our friends at Falaise. The door across the passage closed and he got to his feet. 'They're not there,' he said. 'They're south of Caen and there is an Englishman with them.'

It must surely be the Major! All would be well. I told Pierre that I would try to get away and make for the rendezvous we had arranged before I took up the post at the school. He said that François and another friend were taking over the buses with the children. Jules and Antoine were determined not to leave Caen without me.

'We will wait here for you,' he said. 'We are working on cables near the school and watching it closely.'

I knew it would be useless to tell them to leave Caen, so I accepted their plan and told Pierre to get out of the school now before the officers came back. I had hidden the map in my dress, and I took it out and was just passing it to him when the staff room door opened and the two Gestapo officers emerged.

'What is that?' demanded the one with the half-circle of flowers on his uniform; he was pointing at the paper in my hand, which was folded but not in an envelope.

In all common sense this should have been one of the most terrifying moments in my life. To my own surprise I felt perfectly calm. I could hear Churchill's voice: 'Remember this, Jay Bee; the Germans never believe the obvious.' I smiled and said without hesitation, 'It's a map, of course - what do you think it is?'

He turned scarlet in the face and raged at me in German. They were both so furious that they never noticed Pierre, who snatched the paper and ran. When the shouting went on the senior S.S. officer appeared, and was told what had happened and what I had said. The S.S. officer did his best to calm the others down, and explained that he had given me permission to send a written message. He asked me why I had said it was a map.

'It was just a joke', I said apologetically. 'I am sorry it misfired.'

He looked bewildered. When it came to jokes he was quite out of his depth. The Gestapo officer glared at me, and I had a feeling he had not finished with me, but I could trust Pierre to be well away with the information. The three officers left, and the day passed without further incident, but I had never known time could pass so slowly. It was June 3rd. The second line of the poem would be read tomorrow.

Next morning I awoke full of hope. Operation Overlord would not be long now. Only one more day to get through, and then the Allies would arrive. I was restless all day. The officers were busy and I could not help wondering why they were keeping me here. They were certainly ignoring me. I hoped they were so busy that they had forgotten me.

Somehow I managed to get through the day, and nine o'clock came. I tuned in to the B.B.C. for the news, put the set under the bed and crawled in after it with a blanket over my head. I did not want the Germans to know that I listened to anything but music.

The news came to an end, and the line was not read.

For a moment I felt a wave of physical fear, but it soon passed and I tried to find a reason for what had happened. Had my information about the tanks delayed invasion? Had the Allies made a last minute change of plans? What I did not know was that the weather had changed and upset the planning. I learnt afterwards that there had been hurried consultations and it was eventually decided to postpone the operation for one day.

Next morning I was again awake early. The soldiers were about, but everything was quiet. The officers were either still asleep or already downstairs. I looked out of the window and saw that they were in the school grounds. They seemed to be on the alert and I thought I heard guns in the distance - very faint, but I was sure it was gunfire. I wondered if it would be possible to get on to the roof in the evening and crawl along to the next roof, and so escape; but on looking at the roofs I realised it was impossible.

The day was uneventful and endless, and I longed for the night. Once more I crawled under the bed with my radio set and listened to the nine o'clock news. This time I was better prepared for disappointment - or so I told myself - and it almost came as a shock to hear:

> *'Blessent mon coeur d'une langueur monotone'*
> Wounds my heart with their weary sameness

Order after order followed, and I knew that the S.H.A.E.F. plan for a general uprising had been put into effect. The orders to put the Colour Plans into operation meant that the Resistance would be springing into action. Those who had arm bands would be putting them on and wearing them with pride. The carnage would be terrible.

I did not go to bed that night. I kept very quiet, and was not disturbed. In the morning I looked out of the window and noticed that the Panzer crews were very busy, and then in the distance I saw what I knew to be gliders. Invasion was here. I went downstairs in hopes of seeing or hearing something and I heard an officer say, 'We cannot move without an order. We must wait.'

The senior officer said, 'We will wait until evening.'

He came over to me and told me they might be leaving the following day. He thanked me for my cooperation and said that he would recommend me to the authorities. That amused me, but quite suddenly I felt sorry for him, because I knew that the greatest armada of all time was on its way to liberate Europe. One hundred and fifty Frenchmen would now be on French soil, and the Jed Boys would be coming in to take over and help the Resistance. The Frenchmen were members of the 2nd Chasseurs Parachute Regiment of France attached to S.A.S. They wore a red beret with the badge of the Cross of Lorraine. Their wish would be granted – to be the first liberating force to land back in France.

Actually, as I heard later, a group of British S.A.S. landed further down the coast fifteen minutes ahead of the French. This would not please the Frenchmen, but after all what are fifteen minutes when you have waited for four years?

The S.A.S were in groups of three to ten men. They were equipped with information about towns, streets and the countryside. They were provided with photographs taken by reconnaissance, and I like to think that I too had helped. Each man carried a survival pack to last at least three days. The packs were thought out down to the last detail. Their contents are worth recording:

Each man carried a compass, field glasses, watch, felt-soled boots, rucksack, sleeping bag, American dagger, camouflaged overalls, parachute overalls, life jacket, explosives, many grenades, phials of morphia, a chemical to confuse dogs, a pullover that when unravelled would make thirty feet of twine strong enough to bear the weight of a man, a small metal saw which could be slipped under a shoulder strap, a battledress button which would pivot on another button to make a compass, a map of France on a silk handkerchief, two banknotes for one thousand francs each which when rolled would fit into a lapel, a Commando pack which contained sufficient food for three days, tablets of chewing gum, cubes of vitamins, cubes of solidified concentrated milk, tablets of bitter chocolate, four pieces of sugar, a small piece of soap, a miniature razor and blade, needle and thread, a file for escape use if caught, and three pieces of toilet paper. The Powers That Be had foreseen every possible contingency.

The liberation of Europe had taken over two years of planning in cooperation with the Allies, as well as the British planning when they held the Germans back alone. Victory was in sight, though there would be many set-backs before it was achieved.

I thought, 'The Panzers will be leaving tomorrow and I shall be free.' But this was not how it turned out. At about 3.30 on the afternoon of June 6th – D-Day – Caen was bombed. We were to see wave after wave of Allied bombers at low level flight bombing Caen and the surrounding district. First of all incendiary bombs were dropped, then two hours later high explosives. The pattern continued until midnight. The Germans could not move from the school. The bombing continued on June 7th and 8th. On the 9th we had a naval bombardment, British ships shelling us from the coast.

I was beginning to despair. The Germans seemed to have forgotten about me. The tanks had been grouped into a block with the crews and officers hiding around them. I could not help thinking how much better it would have been if they had dispersed their tanks about the grounds. I slept upstairs, but came down to my office during the day; I did not want to be on the top floor if the school was hit. It was now June 10th and since Invasion Day I had been living on vitamin tablets and any food I could scrounge from the kitchen during raids, when the soldiers were sheltering. The tablets were those issued for survival, and thanks to the Major's foresight I had a good supply with me this time.

That day explosive bombs hit the school and part of the roof caved in, but to my great delight Pierre managed to reach me unseen by the Germans. He had brought a sack for my receiving and transmitting set. The stairs were gritty with fallen plaster but we crept up, our feet crunching in the debris, and found my bedroom intact. I put on as many clothes as I could, in order to leave space in my suitcase for food, and as soon as the next wave of bombers arrived we went down to the kitchen. As we had hoped, it was deserted – the soldiers had all sought shelter. We filled the case up with food, I picked it up, Pierre shouldered the sack and we slipped out as the bombs were falling.

I felt very heavy with so many clothes on; it was a warm day and the air was full of smoke and dust. The streets were a terrible sight. They were littered with dead bodies. The only living people we saw were trying, like ourselves, to escape from the town. Pierre led the way to where Antoine was waiting for us with a car. He said that Jules was busy sabotaging the railways. A little south of Caen he stopped the car and we parked it in a wood. Pierre and Antoine were anxious to tell me everything that had happened.

Pierre said that on June 6th the skies had opened and hundreds of pieces of equipment had come down - Bren and Sten guns, grenades, anti-tank rifles, etc. As the Resistance gathered the weapons in, many of them were killed by the Germans, but there were always others to take their place so that the Germans could not get the equipment. Men and women alike were proud to wear the arm band. Although they knew that the Germans would kill them on sight, they were so eager for arm bands that they even took them off their dead comrades.

Antoine said that the Colour Plans had been put into operation. Trains had been derailed or blown up, and some two thousand were prevented from moving; cars had been stopped and destroyed. Post and telegraph workers - Pierre among them - had destroyed the secret cable that the Germans had laid, so that communications were slowed down. They told me that many buildings in Caen had been destroyed, but so far the Abbaye had not been hit. It was packed with people who had sought shelter there and would not leave. When the raids were over the Abbaye was still untouched and the people safe. Later I learnt that the French Resistance had got a message through to General Montgomery at Allied H.Q. at Bayeux, telling him that hundreds of civilians were taking shelter in the Abbaye. As a result the low-flying bombers were careful to avoid it.

Pierre said that he wondered why it was necessary for Caen to be so heavily bombed. I told him I did not know, but in my own mind I could picture what had happened. I realised that, because the raid started in the afternoon of June 6th, Montgomery must have received my information about the position of Rommel's tanks. If the Caen area had not been so heavily bombed, Rommel could have moved his tanks to the coast immediately on his recall from Paris - he got back in the evening of June 6th - and he would have collided head-on with Montgomery. The outcome of the invasion might then have been very different.

I asked Pierre whether he had had any difficulty in making

contact with the Falaise friends. He said that everything had gone as planned and the Englishman had asked him to give me a message. It was: 'The Major says thank you.' Somehow I had been sure the Major would be near at hand to receive information direct.

We returned to sleep in the wood each night and during the day we did all we could to help the refugees. Many people were trying to escape to the south, and Pierre and Antoine provided transport; they always seemed to know where they could get hold of vehicles. Pierre said that he had taken some elderly friends of Jules to the Fleury Caves near Caen, and also our friends from Evreux, which I was very glad to hear. The caves provided shelter for a great many people.

Rommel put up a good fight. Before the end there was fierce hand-to-hand fighting in the streets of Caen and in the area from the coast to Falaise. The last big raid was on July 9th and the break-through came on July 15th, when we saw the Americans. During the raids the Malherbe School became a hospital. The refectory was used as an operating theatre; over eight thousand air raid victims were treated and many others died of their injuries. Some were buried in the courtyards.

Apart from the Abbaye, the centre of Caen was completely destroyed; over thirty-five thousand people died and thousands were injured. The industries of the town were either destroyed or badly damaged. After hostilities ceased the French took advantage of the destruction to rebuild Caen in a modern style which is much admired. Their industries are now between the river, the canal and the sea. The church of St Pierre has been restored and the utter devastation of 1944 wiped out. Life must go on, and it is good to improve on the past.

The soldiers of the Wehrmacht were surrendering everywhere. It was said afterwards that over two hundred thousand Germans were taken prisoner, including twenty generals. The Himmler S.S. Panzer detachment at the school met with the same fate - it was probably lucky for them that they were unable to move out their tanks. Rommel was wounded, but escaped to fight on.

24

Aftermath

On July 17th, when the raids had ceased and the area was clear of Germans, we went to the Fleury caves to make sure the people knew it was now safe to come out, and to give them what help we could. The conditions there were terrible. Many of them had taken refuge there on June 6th. No one had realised they would have to stay for so long; food supplies had run out, and even water was so short that they had been reduced to getting moisture from the stalactites that dripped from the cave roof.

When the people, mainly elderly, came out of the caves, they were met by a sight of frightful devastation. Decomposing bodies were rotting in the hot July sun. The stench was unbearable and many began to vomit. Among the rotting dead flowering anemones of every colour were pushing their way up and I hoped they felt, as I did, that God had not deserted them. Here was new life, new hope that France would rise again. Old men, women and young children fell to their knees in prayer, tears streaming down their cheeks as their fingers counted their rosaries.

I shall never forget this scene. If any one picture were needed to show the tragic, pointless waste of war, this one should serve the purpose.

Our friends from Evreux were badly shaken by their experiences. Their farm lay on the direct route between Caen and Paris; it had been overrun, and they were not sure what to do. I advised them to come south with us. I told them I had friends at the small seaside resort of Guethary, where I felt sure they would be welcome. They asked if it was near Hendaye as they had relations living there. They were delighted to hear that it was only a few miles away, and became more composed. I told them that further south we would pass them over to a group who would take them to either their friends or mine.

We made our way south to the rendezvous where we were to meet Jules, François and Georges. Jules had a message for me from the Major, telling me to be at the doctor's house at Limoges on July 30th. Jules had been in the Lyon area a few days before meeting us, to try to find some of his friends, many of whom were resisting the Germans there. He found that many of his comrades had been killed. The Germans seemed to be killing anything that moved. Communist Resistance was also active, chasing the Militia and rounding up anyone who had collaborated with the Germans. Jules said he was sure that many members of the Militia had taken off their uniforms now that the Germans were on the run. He said there had been a massacre at Vercors only a few days previously, and Jules was in tears as he told me of it.

The Resistance at Vercors had asked for help to deal with the Germans as they had very little equipment to fight with, and they were assured that this would be sent, together with leaders from Algiers. Eventually planes arrived and they saw what they thought were Allied soldiers coming down by parachute. They ran out to meet them, only to find that they were Germans. Not only did these Germans kill everything they could see, they also raped and tortured women and girls. They overran the Plateau, burning buildings and killing.

The Third Reich S.S. together with the Waffen S.S. committed untold atrocities. They were unable to contact Allied troops and when harassed by the Resistance groups they retaliated on the civilian population. Jules was very bitter, and said that the communication between the Gaullist groups and American O.S.S. in Algiers was bad. Liaison was weak; many Gaullist groups did not understand English and many O.S.S. leaders did not understand French, so they could not communicate. This may or may not be true. Human errors do occur, and it was a fact that many innocent people died.

The men told me of the massacre of Oradour-sur-Glave. The Resistance had fought some of the Third Reich S.S. Division at Oradour-sur-Vayres and a Commander had been killed. The rest of the S.S. Division retaliated by going to the other village of a similar name, where they thought the Commander had been killed, and the people of Oradour-sur-Glave became the victims of this error. The Germans shot every man and boy, then shut the women, girls and young children in the church and set fire to it. One woman survived; this was a miracle, because armed S.S. Germans surrounded the church to make sure that no one escaped alive.

On hearing this, I felt an intense hatred of the Germans, but I also hated myself because I could not suppress the emotion. Hatred is self-destructive. You cannot live decently with hate in your heart.

It was now July 25th and we made our way to Limoges, where we were in time for the memorial service being held there for the victims of the Oradour-sur-Glave massacre. The men accompanied me to the service, together with our Evreux friends. The Mayor of Limoges, in his address, said, 'Let us not hate the Germans for their atrocities. Let us pity them, for they will have to live with these horrors on their conscience. They will never be allowed to forget, but let us try to forgive them.' I do not think the congregation were impressed. It was too near home and too soon for forgiveness; but I knew in my heart that he was right, and I felt some of the hate within myself beginning to leave me.

I met the Major at the doctor's house in Limoges where we had been nailed up in the cellar. I had not realised until now that the doctor was such an active member of Resistance. He certainly had not shown any sign of this to us, although we knew that he was sympathetic to the movement and helped its members whenever possible. I told the Major we had his friends from Evreux with us and we wanted to get them as near as possible to Hendaye, and he said he would take them with him on his way to the coast. They were delighted to see him, all the more so when they learnt that he would get them to Hendaye. This town is on the coast, on the Spanish border. Guethary is quite near, and I told them that if there were any difficulties in Hendaye they could go to my friends, who had a small hotel.

I noticed that our Evreux friends also referred to 'The Major' and did not use a surname. It seemed that I was never to know his name, even through other people.

I arranged to meet the Major at Tarbes in August, when he would take me back to England. I told him that I was anxious to get my men to the south, and if they were willing I would leave them with friends of mine at La Turbie, just north of Monte Carlo. I thought it better to get them away, as Communist groups were taking reprisals against people who had not joined with them, and in many groups were trying to get some sort of power. My men had not told me anything of this, but I had heard Jules and Antoine talking when they were unaware that I could hear them, and I had gathered from their conversation that they were confused. Personally, I had always thought of them as left-wing trades unionists. They had considered themselves French

Communists, but were no longer in sympathy with this line of thought. They had changed a great deal since I had met them. They were disgusted at the way the Communists were behaving and might be termed traitors by their former friends. They would be safe at La Turbie and would be welcome to stay there until hostilities ceased, or for as long as they wished.

The Major said the S.A.S. were doing splendid work in mopping up and taking over several Resistance groups. The Jed Boys were also rounding up groups and trying to get some kind of order amongst them.

After he and the Evreux people had left us, we drove south, making for Toulouse. Georges had friends there whom he wanted to contact. We kept off the National route; we made good headway and managed to get food and drink on the way. We saw a great deal of damage, the result of the Resistance chasing the German troops north so that the Americans could deal with them. When we got nearer to Toulouse we saw signs of fighting, as the Americans had taken over the task of defeating the Germans in the South and Midi.

After the break-through from Normandy, the British and Canadians were ordered north; General Patton's army dealt with the rest. The Germans were on the run and demoralised. General Elster of the Third Reich was trying to reach Nevers and hoped that he could get home to Germany that way, but he could not escape. The American Third Army was verging south and the troops of the Free French Army, who had landed on the Mediterranean coast, were behind him. Resistance harassed his troops the whole time. They ambushed them in woods, bridges were blown up and explosives placed on roads. The Germans retaliated. They fired at anyone they saw and burned and pillaged as they went. They took reprisals against the local population; practically every village the Germans passed through suffered promiscuous carnage. There were about 2,000 S.A.S. and Resistance chasing some 18,000 to 20,000 Germans. The odds were great, but the Germans never knew just where attacks would come from. The Resistance drove them towards General Patton's armies, but hoped that they themselves would be able to take over the surrender. It would have meant a great deal to their morale and would have compensated for some of the sufferings they had endured as Resistance members of groups in hiding for over two years.

They were not to have this satisfaction. The Germans under

General Elster surrendered to the Americans at Beaugency, and the Resistance members had the unfortunate experience of seeing the Americans giving their German prisoners chocolate and oranges - commodities that they had not seen for years. Feelings ran high. The French showed a great deal of understandable bitterness, but serious trouble was eventually avoided. The American general who took the surrender had only been in Europe for three months. How could he have known of the many atrocities committed by General Elster's army? He was trying to be compassionate towards a defeated enemy. One cannot judge without knowing all the circumstances.

A great many American troops had landed on the coast and were arriving from the south. We avoided them if we could. We were never questioned, but if we had been I had a special pass given to me by the Major, who had told me to use it only in an extreme emergency.

As we neared Toulouse we stopped in a wooded area near a village. We noticed a lot of flies near a tree and went to see what was attracting them. To our horror we saw, propped against a tree, the bodies of two young girls. They could not have been more than fifteen years of age. They were naked and their stomachs had been slit open. One had her intestines hanging about her neck.

My men had all killed without a qualm. I had not killed, but I had authorised killing. Countless of our friends and helpers had been butchered, many had been tortured. In the last few weeks the sight of death had become commonplace. We had thought that we were hardened to anything. Now we discovered that we were not. Pierre dashed away and we heard him vomiting. Jules and Georges stood where they were and cursed quietly, endlessly. Antoine just stared, like someone in a trance. I was frozen. I could not move, and my blood seemed to be literally running cold. My limbs were completely stiff, as if I had been standing for hours in a snowstorm. At last Antoine's voice came through to me - Antoine who always knew what to do and did it without fuss. He said pathetically, 'What do we do?'

His words dragged me back to reality. I said, 'We bury them.'

The suggestion of action brought the men back to life. I said, 'We can make a shallow grave and put the bodies in. Then one of you must go to the village and find the priest and tell him what we have done.'

Pierre rejoined us and offered to go for the priest. By the time he returned with the priest and another man we had done what we could with the tools we possessed. We showed them the grave, and they told us of the rape and carnage the people of the village had suffered. We left them and went on to Toulouse.

We reached Toulouse safely the same evening. We had never had any difficulty about petrol. The men seemed to get it quite easily, so I did not ask questions. We had never been short of food on this journey either, but it had been very monotonous, mainly bread. Georges' friends had a small hotel where we were able to have a bath, which was a real luxury. The food we had brought from the school was long since eaten, so I had all my luggage in my suitcase. I felt sorry for the men as they had very little clothing with them, but Georges' friends helped with this. They made a great fuss over us and prepared a truly magnificent feast. I would not have believed that we could do justice to it after our recent experience, but in fact we all tucked in and enjoyed ourselves, and were soon laughing and joking with our hosts.

We were not insensitive. All the horrors that we had heard about or witnessed had left a mark on us that would never quite fade, but fortunately human beings have a built-in mechanism that prevents their brooding on the unbearable. The same reaction could be seen among the soldiers in the field and the people at home at the height of the blitz - in the midst of horror there was humour, and humour saved our sanity.

It was a meal to remember. We began with *soupe garbure*, which is made from vegetables in which a goose leg is simmered; this was followed by river trout; then we had lean duck steak with mushrooms, petits pois and Toulouse sausages. There was a great deal of fruit to choose from - sweet chestnuts, grapes, strawberries, peaches. We had Pyrenean wine and finished with the violet liqueur of Toulouse. After this banquet and a happy, sociable evening we were invited to stay the night and gladly accepted.

I thought it was time we began to plan for the future. I told the men I wanted to be in Tarbes by the end of August, and suggested that they should go to my friends in La Turbie. However, they decided to stay for the present in Toulouse. I confessed that I had overheard their conversation and knew that they were afraid their Communist friends would look on them as traitors. They said they no longer held any political views. They just wanted to be good French citizens. They wanted to settle down and forget, if possible, the fighting and killing. They had endured enough.

The owners of the hotel said they could stay with them for the time being. Jules thought he might get back his job as Railway

Inspector when France had settled down, and Pierre and François could return to post and telegraph. Georges wanted to go back to Marseille as soon as it was possible. There would be plenty of work on the docks. I gave them the address of my friends in La Turbie, also an address in Monte Carlo and another in Nice. A letter to any of these places would reach me in England. I insisted that they must contact me in any emergency - I was not as sanguine about their future as they appeared to be, and time proved me right.

They said they would drive me to Tarbes. We stayed together at the hotel until it was time to set out, and I left money with Georges' friends to repay them for their hospitality. We saw much destruction on the way to Tarbes, but the villa belonging to our Portuguese friends was unharmed. We were all made very welcome there and the men were offered jobs, if they ever needed them, at the Hispano-Suiza factory in which our host had an interest. They promised to bear it in mind.

I was staying on in Tarbes to await the Major's arrival, and the men were returning to Toulouse. The time had come to part company. When we said *au revoir* it was with the promise to meet the following year, or earlier if circumstances permitted. I asked them if they had enough money and made them promise that if they needed more they would let me know. They embraced me, and I thought yet again how lucky I was to have had such fine men to work with. We had sheltered in woods together, spent nights sleeping rough, faced discomfort, danger and death. A very strong bond united us, forged by mutual trust and respect, and out of this had grown a deep affection. We had all changed, or perhaps it would be truer to say, developed. Pierre in particular; he was much quieter, more thoughtful. Behind the façade of cynicism he was very sensitive and compassionate. He no longer mocked 'me and my God'.

I got in touch with my friends in Monte Carlo and told them about the men. They promised to give them help if they needed it. They were glad to hear from me and know I was safe, but what on earth was I doing in France at this time? I said I was in the Army but did not go into details. Towards the end of August the Major arrived in Tarbes. We left two days later and returned to England in a Hudson. We did not land at Tempsford. This fact in itself brought home to me that my war was over.

The big war, the war of battles and diplomacy, had still a long course to run, but the end was in sight.

25

'Let Yours Be Truthful'

Now at last I had time to reflect on all that had happened.

I made a full report on the siege of Caen and the bravery of her people. Whatever they had done before, the people of Caen rose up as one when their country needed them. The siege of Caen and the death of so many civilians was a tragic affair, but it could not have been avoided. I thought of the Mayor of Caen and his wife who had helped the Resistance during the siege, and of Pierre Rochat, the Sub-Prefect of Bayeux; he had been the ideal civil servant, carrying on as best he could under occupation for the benefit of the people. Yet how quickly these loyal Frenchmen were removed by General de Gaulle and replaced by his own men from Algiers.

I could not help feeling sorry for the aged Marshal Pétain. I am sure he capitulated to the Germans to save the people of Paris. He believed Hitler when he said there would be no interference with the Vichy government, and there were many traitors in France at that time who encouraged him in this belief. The Marshal was a soldier, not a politician. On D-Day he made a passionate call to the French, urging them to help the Allies in every way possible. I do not think he was a traitor to France. He believed that he could save the people of France only by sacrificing France. The result was a disaster for both land and people. De Gaulle, on the other hand, was prepared to sacrifice French lives in order to save France. In my opinion both men were patriots, each in his own way.

After hostilities ended many people in France jumped on the band-wagon. The General went round the country giving out medals and certificates to many who had resisted, but also to many who had not, and even to some who had secretly collaborated with the Germans. It is sad to reflect how often nations do not recognise their real heroes and heroines. Many of our own S.O.E. were offered civil awards instead of military ones; many of them refused these medals.

I reflected also on the German generals of the Wehrmacht who remained unaffected by the poison of Nazism. I thought of the general who left Rome with his troops so that the city was saved from destruction, and of the general who surrendered to the Gaullist Resistance leader rather than destroy Paris. I feel strongly about giving credit where it is due, even though these men were fighting against us. We should not judge them too harshly; they were professional soldiers and had nothing in common with the men of the Nazi Party. But how could a cultured race such as the Germans be fooled by madmen such as Hitler and Goebbels - they were for years.

I reflected how fortunate the people of the United Kingdom were in having so many good leaders - Admirals, Generals and Air Marshals. Politicians too were able to work together with a common purpose; in the National Government, they could rise above their individual Party. I am sure there is a lesson to be learnt from this.

Above all, we were fortunate in our own people. We British were at our best during those dark, difficult years. We can do almost anything if we have the will to do it, although it is strange that we have to be brought to our knees before we are roused. When we know that something must be done, we do not stop until we have completed the task.

The Germans were not defeated yet. They would continue to fight in their own country, and we had to face many setbacks. The first of the flying bombs had hit this country in June, and the Germans produced an even fiercer and more destructive weapon in the flying rocket. We were eventually able to counter these menaces by destroying the launching sites and also the bombs in flight.

The German scientists had certainly progressed beyond any other country in their knowledge of space-craft. On the defeat of Germany, America invited - or took - German space scientists to America, and Russia invited - or took - others to work in Russia, which resulted in the space race which started in each country after the war. Let us hope that eventually they will share their knowledge for the benefit of mankind.

I did not see Winston Churchill again until 1945. It was in May, just before Victory in Europe was celebrated. He had been shattered when General Montgomery was made to halt near

Berlin. 'We have been dishonoured', said Churchill brokenly. He looked as though he had aged ten years in a single night. Americans had Supreme Command and did not seem to realise that we were failing the people of Poland. France and Great Britain had signed a pact with Poland in 1939 to aid them and the time had come when it was possible to do so.

Churchill asked me what I now intended to do, and said that he could arrange for me to go on German Control, to deal with displaced persons in Germany. I did not want to do this; I had finished what was expected of me, and now I wanted to forget the horrors of war; to go where I could see something of nature, to see things growing. Later on I would go back to France, as I had arranged to meet my Lyon group. I would also try to get in touch with my other groups, to find out whether they were in need of help, and see that their services to their country were suitably rewarded.

I was not altogether successful in this latter project. I had always been careful to know as little as possible of their private lives, and now in some cases it was impossible to make contact. Also records had been destroyed - deliberately, I am afraid, in some cases, out of jealousy and malice. These were some of the people who were never repaid by France for their self-sacrifice on her behalf. Churchill told me I could keep the Sloane Street flat for as long as I wished. The 'Secret Place' was to be closed down at the end of hostilities. In the Autumn of 1945 the lights went out and who better to do this than George Rance; only a few knew George and his skill in making everyone comfortable at Storey's Gate. His hero was Churchill.

The Prime Minister was to visit the Allied Troops in Europe to congratulate them on victory and I was delighted to have seen him before his departure; I understood that on his return he would be staying at Claridges. It was General Election year. The Prime Minister continued to say to me that he was sorry I would not accept the offer to serve on control in Germany - he said I could then have the honours I deserved. I told him I did not want honours for myself. I was a democrat and had my own philosophy and tried to live up to it. I said how privileged I felt to have been of service to my country through him. Some day I hoped to write a book so that people could know of his Secret Circle, if the time ever came when it could be made known. He said, 'You will have to wait at least twenty years before you can say anything about your work with the Circle. I shall probably be dead by then so shall not have to answer any awkward questions. Be careful when you write not to mention names or individual buildings, just towns and areas. People have to live on, and must try to forget where Germans committed their atrocities. People can become morbid about the past, and places can be made features of morbid interest. You can mention some people of course, at your discretion, especially if it will be to their benefit.' He smiled at me – 'Others will undoubtedly write books. They will write fiction and non-fiction and near fiction – I ask only one thing Jay Bee, let yours be truthful.' I promised that, if ever I did write my book, I would write only the truth, and this I have now done to the best of my ability. This is not a work of fiction or even near-fiction. It is a true account of the years I spent as a member of the Secret Circle. If I have made any mistakes in writing about events which did not directly concern me, I have done so involuntarily. I have made every effort to check my facts.

I told Churchill that it had been a wonderful experience being in his Secret Circle. I said that I still did not know the Major's name.

He said, 'Believe me, it is for the best reasons that you do not know it.' He stood up and put out his hand to shake mine. 'Goodbye, sir,' I said.

He looked sad and tired, but he gripped my hand warmly and said, 'Thank you, Jay Bee, for your loyalty. It is something that money cannot buy.' With his words ringing in my ears, I left Storey's Gate for the last time.

During the last year of the war I had been able to enjoy some social life again. My cousin was out of London, but I could now see my father and my friends. It was a great pleasure to stay with friends in the country, but I also spent some time at the flat. I met a great many American Service people, and I also saw the Major on many occasions. I had not seen him for some time when I visited Churchill at Storey's Gate, but a week later he came to see me.

I thought he looked very tired. It had been a long war, and there was still work to be done. He said he was sorry I would not be going to Germany, but quite understood my feelings about it. He asked after Jo, and was surprised to hear that she had joined the Land Army as an officer. He said that he would like to meet me in July if I was still in London.

This date was duly kept, and when we met he told me he would be leaving London and we would probably never meet again. I asked him if he was in the Army, but he said he was sorry, he could

not tell me anything about himself. The following day we met at
the flat and went to the House of Commons to see Winston
Churchill. He had left Storey's Gate and moved to Claridges. The
General Election was over and the Labour Party had come to
power. We both told Churchill how sorry we were that he was out
of office, and I said, 'You are not forgotten, sir, and never will be.'
(When Downing Street was hit by bombs an apartment was used
by the Prime Minister at Storey's Gate but in May 1945 he moved
out as the annexe was no longer to be used. Victory in Europe was
being celebrated. The P.M. was leaving London for Europe to
attend the many Victory marches and to visit both British and
Allied troops. He received almost a snub from British troops.
Small wonder! The opposition had begun their election
campaign - the forces were promised much from them - when
election came in July it was a landslide - and Labour won on a
Forces vote.)

The impish look came into his eyes. I had not seen it there for a
long time. 'If they have forgotten me now,' he said, 'they will not
do so when I die, for I shall have the biggest state funeral that this
country has ever seen; and if Norfolk is still in charge and does
not make a good job of it, I shall come back and haunt him!'

He shook hands with us. We were all laughing as we said
goodbye. On the way out we met Ernie Bevin and he stopped us.

I said, 'You are not supposed to know us! It's still a secret.'

'I know,' he replied, 'but I just had to say how much I learnt
from the Old Boy. It was a wonderful time. I am back on the other
side now, but I shall always remember. We are political
opponents but the friendship is still there underneath and it will
remain there.'

That evening the Major took me to dine at Claridges. It was
very enjoyable, but I knew that it was a 'last meal' - even though
we did not have bacon and eggs. He escorted me back to the flat,
kissed my hand and left. I have never seen him since and I still do
not know his name.

There were many things of which I saw a part but never learnt
the whole, but many other things that were Top Secret have now
become public knowledge. Among these I am glad that the full
story of the Enigma has now come to light. Owing to the secrecy
that surrounded it, there are many men and women whose magnificent work in this field could not be given due recognition. Now at
last their names can be made known. Some of them are no longer
alive to receive our thanks; let us at least honour their memory.

Our possession of the machine which we named the Enigma was the most vital and best-kept secret of the whole war. It enabled us to decode Hitler's orders to his generals and all Goering's orders to his Command. It was a bonus to the commands of all our Services. As it was absolutely essential that the Germans should never know or have the faintest suspicion that we had this machine in our possession, the decoding carried out at Bletchley was referred to as the 'Ultra System' and very few outside Bletchley knew the truth. The men and women who worked there were nicknamed the 'Bletchley Boys and Girls'. They were among the very best brains in the country - university dons, mathematicians, linguists, chess experts - and we owe them a great debt of gratitude.

Their story is not my story - I hope that one day it will be written - but I cannot end without making mention of some of the outstanding code breakers of Bletchley. I would like to see their names on a special Roll of Honour, whether they be dead or alive.

Alistair Denniston, the man who brought the Enigma out of Poland is now dead. He was one of our greatest code breakers, but little credit has been given to him. Group Captain Winterbottom was retired as a Group Captain, but I feel sure that if all had been known he would have had higher rank. Dilly Knox killed himself with overwork; he was a sick man and knew that time was precious, but he spent the time left to him at this exacting task. Admiral Sir Hugh Sinclair was another who died without seeing the final results of his work. Oliver Strachey, a gifted musician, also possessed a brilliant mathematical brain. Dr R. V. Jones, who further bent the radar beam, gave up other important work to devote himself to service which he knew could never receive public recognition. He is still alive and giving his knowledge to students at a Scottish university. Any student who has the privilege to attend this 'Beam Man's' lectures is very fortunate. To Colonel Menzies we owe more than we ever guessed for his work on the Ultra System and Defence. Lord Swinton, Air Minister after Londonderry, gave tremendous help to the Air Force Commanders.

To these and many other unsung heroes and heroines of the Back Room we owe the security of our lives today.

Among the many successes to which the Enigma vitally contributed was that of General Auchinleck. His foreknowledge of Hitler's intentions, together with his own skill, enabled him to stop Rommel at the gates of Egypt. Had this not happened we would have lost the Mediterranean – perhaps for ever.

But possibly the most important message intercepted through Enigma was Hitler's order to Goering before the Battle of Britain. It was: 'Get all the British fighters in the air at once. Destroy the aircraft in the air and destroy the airfields.' It was for this reason that a small handful of fighters had to bear the brunt of the attack alone. Churchill never believed that there would be an invasion from the sea. Our aircraft were vital to our defence, and our Air Force was still not up to strength. He therefore gave the order to Air Marshal Lord Dowding to keep a large proportion of fighters in reserve; we just could not afford to throw them all into battle and risk losing them. Many fighters were hidden away in secret airfields while cardboard planes took their place on the runways and were destroyed.

After the Battle, an inquiry was called by the Air Marshal's junior staff to ask why all fighter squadrons had not been put into service. Lord Dowding could give no adequate explanation without betraying the secret of our inside information. He was demoted to Coastal Command and had to face much adverse criticism in his lifetime. Now that the secrecy has been lifted I hope that full credit will be given to the memory of this honourable and courageous man. Churchill always intended that the Enigma would be a secret forever but it was made known in 1975.

I kept in touch with my Paris friends and the men of my Lyon group and visited them several times. Jacques died in 1952. Marie and he remained good friends but never married. The Lyon group, including Georges, all married and all but Pierre had children. Jules and François returned to their old jobs and were quite content in them. Jules died in 1957. Pierre, Antoine and Georges found work of various kinds but never seemed to get satisfactorily settled. They were unpopular with the Gaullists because they had been Communists, and with the Communists because they were looked upon as renegades. In 1963 I had a letter from François asking if I could help these three, who were having a difficult time. I found that what they really wanted was to settle down and farm, to be independent and to forget the war years. I had every sympathy with this ambition. I remembered that when I returned to England in 1944 my dearest wish had been to see things grow. I managed to help them to get smallholdings in the Basses-Pyrénées. They did not know much about farming, but with hard work and good advice they have become self-supporting and enjoy the life.

They were later joined by Alex, another ex-Maquisard who had been of help to several of my groups. Alex was a genius at concocting and using explosives. His special forte was blowing up bridges, which he did as casually as Vincent had planted grenades among his cabbages. I have seen him pass the time of day with a German sentry on a bridge moments before it was due to go up.

Alex was a raconteur. Among his anecdotes of the Resistance my favourite, which has nothing to do with explosives, is the episode of the 'grey mice'. This was the nickname the French gave to the German nurses, who wore a grey uniform. A group with which Alex was working at the time had captured a German lorry, killing the driver. To their embarrassment they found that its load consisted of a batch of frightened 'grey mice' on their way to report for work at a German Army Camp. While the puzzled men were arguing about what to do with their catch, the problem was settled by the girls, who begged to be taken with them and allowed to work for the Maquis. The French Maquisards and the German nurses, who were simple, uncomplicated country girls, settled down very happily together in the forest, leading a Robin Hood existence, the men carrying out their acts of brigandage and the girls cooking and washing for them. This went on until a Resistance leader turned up and insisted that they send the girls away. The men protested indignantly, the girls wept and pleaded: 'Please don't send us back to the Germans! We want to stay and work for you.' The leader had to give way. The girls stayed, and after the war they married their captors and became good French wives and mothers.

In 1973, after the death of his wife, Pierre joined a Benedictine order. I do not know whether Pierre found God or God found Pierre, but the sceptic is now devoted to his faith.

To look back at the past is to stir up mixed emotions. It is to feel some pain, some sadness and regret; but it is also to relive moments of laughter and times of quiet contentment, especially the happiness that only friendship can give. All experiences are a part of life, and life is good.

My experiences in the war have taught me much. From brutality I learnt mercy; from starvation and want I learnt generosity; from failure and humiliation I learnt leadership and a great faith in God and in my fellow men. Above all I learnt that, much as I appreciate the freedom of communication through books and newspapers and the wonders of radio and television, the best communication is between people.

I have had a wonderful life. I have stayed in the best hotels in England and on the Continent. I have lived in stately homes, and on my lecture tours I have enjoyed the hospitality of family houses and flats. I have hidden in woods and ditches. I have used beautifully appointed bathrooms and washed in streams. I have eaten superb meals and have been grateful for stale cabbage leaves and what I could scrape up from the fields. I have slept in luxurious beds, on the bare ground, in cellars, in a Gestapo prison and once in a hollow tree.

In fact, I have lived.

Epilogue

On January 24th, 1965, the great heart of Winston Leonard Spencer Churchill ceased to beat. He had endeared himself to those in every land who loved freedom. He was a man who filled many roles: soldier, writer, artist, traveller, orator and statesman. His vision of Europe and the world was something few men ever had. He knew success, failure and humiliation. Meanness and pettiness were alien to his nature.

Hitler hated him because he knew that Churchill hated all tyrants and dictators. From 1934 until the actual outbreak of war Churchill's was a lone voice crying out warnings against the ruthless advance of Nazism. But when war became a reality it was to him that the people of Britain turned. In 1940 he heartened us with a firm resolve when he stated, 'We shall never surrender. There is only one answer to defeat and that is victory.' In our darkest hours his voice became the voice of the people of Britain, putting into simple, stirring words the feelings that we could not ourselves express.

He walked with kings and commoners alike. He loved the monarchy and could not conceive of us without a monarch. He helped us to remember with pride all that is best in the British way of life, and inspired us to maintain that way of life: freedom of thought, speech and action within the laws of the land, and the courage to say 'no' to those who seek to undermine our freedom. He had faith in the nation's ability to overcome all difficulties and he was the inspiration of all who fought in secret in the cause of freedom against tyranny, law against violence, mercy against inhumanity.

In 1939 this country had little to fight with except dogged determination. We were disastrously short of orthodox weapons to combat the vast armaments our enemies had been piling up. As Churchill had foreseen, we would have to use unorthodox weapons.

A new ministry was formed in London, the Ministry of Economic Warfare. A large block of luxury flats in Berkeley Square became the home of the greatest Think Tank ever conceived, where men and women of the highest intellectual calibre and most expert specialised knowledge pooled their brains to fight war on economic lines and 'hit the enemy where it hurt most'. I had the blessing of Neville Chamberlain and afterwards of Winston Churchill. The first Minister was Hugh Dalton, a member of the National Government of the day and a member of the Labour Party. At the time that I worked there the Minister was Lord Selbourne.

Before the war a Major Holland had talked and written about a new kind of warfare. He declared that future wars would be fought differently. Groups of men of five, ten, and up to twenty could do more damage working in secret as a force of saboteurs than could hundreds of soldiers. Most Service leaders were not interested, but among the few who were was Winston Churchill. When he came to power as Prime Minister and Minister of Defence in May 1940 he told Hugh Dalton to 'set Europe alight with saboteurs' and to keep the Germans harassed. Special forces came into being and men and women were chosen from these to form S.O.E. (Special Operations Executive).

This new type of warfare needed men and women of exceptional qualities. They had to have tremendous self-discipline; they had to maintain a normal way of life and yet carry out secret tasks. They were chosen for their ability to have no qualms of conscience in carrying out these secret missions and not to question the legality of their actions. They had to have the capacity for patience and silence, the control never to act recklessly or impulsively. They were men and women who had strong beliefs and were willing to undergo arduous training in this new warfare. Their patriotism went hand in hand with a very special kind of courage.

S.O.E. was to be a subversive force of sabotage, forming underground armies to work in secret against a powerful enemy. It was not a political or intelligence service.

General de Gaulle did not welcome the idea of Resistance groups. He favoured an Intelligence Force in France to let him know how affairs stood in that country. There were however Frenchmen who desired a practical form of resistance, and I think one can fairly say that the first organised resistance came from General Cochet (retired Air Force). He sent letters written by himself to be dropped through letter boxes of officers and other men whom he knew, asking them to resist in any way they could. The Cochet Letters became an inspiration to many Frenchmen. He told people to put German cars out of action by pouring sugar into petrol tanks, and to defy the Germans whenever possible. He begged the French to support the Allies in every way in their power. Many responded to his appeal; even children climbed telegraph poles to cut down wires. The Marquis de Moustier blew up some of his own mines so that the Germans would not get the minerals, especially coal. He lost four million pounds in doing so.

The Germans tried to establish groups to teach the 'New Order', groups which they would be able to manipulate. French people formed opposing groups, 'Liberties', 'Peasants and Workers' and others. Many Communists were arrested in France at the outbreak of war, as Germany and Russia had signed a neutrality pact, so at first the Communists sat on the fence. However, when Germany declared war on Russia in 1941 the Communists became very keen resisters. The Communist Maquis served the country well against Nazi Germany, but they came to realise that Resistance was a power which could be used to take over countries after hostilities had ceased. Fortunately there were people in Britain who feared this, and a Prime Minister who foresaw the danger and acted accordingly.

At first all the different resistance groups in occupied countries were not sufficiently organised to do very much harm, but it was a beginning. They met to discuss the Germans and methods of harassing them. The various movements were planting the seeds, so that when help came from Britain they would prove to be a harvest for the liberation of Europe.

In the new kind of warfare organised by the British, the brains of officers whose names were to become famous - Gubbins, Boddington and Buckmaster - were used to build up an organisation of a few against many. Numerous mistakes were made and they were up against the jealousy of others, a weakness of human nature which we all have to face at some time. There were many deaths, but this was a price which those serving in this force were prepared to pay. The three officers I have named and their staff were based in Baker Street and became known to their colleagues at the War Office and to M.E.W. as the 'Baker Street Boys'.

It can be said that the Resistance Movement's greatest

contribution to victory was that it kept the flame of freedom burning.

I never belonged to any officially organised Resistance movement. My work and that of my groups was unknown to any government. But I had the privilege of working for my country under the leadership of Winston Churchill and under the dedicated direction of the Major; I met many wonderful people, from the most brilliant brains in this country to the humblest workers and peasants of France, all of whom where in some way involved in this unorthodox war.

Since I have been able to break silence and speak of my experiences I have often been asked, 'Was it worth all the sacrifice? So many people died, the young airmen, soldiers, sailors, the Resistance groups and their leaders, and all the civilians, the men, women and children. Look at the world today. Has it improved?'

Of course it was worth it! We fought for freedom, and we fought for peace. There is a challenge each time that freedom is threatened and we must face the challenge. We must not forget that tyranny is a disease. We may think we have rooted it out, but it is a virus which can attack again at any time and in any place. The challenge remains today. Do we really value this freedom which we owe to the countless men and women who gave their lives to keep the flame burning? What part as individuals are we playing in continuing to carry that torch worldwide?

I believe in our young people of today. They may, through sheer youthful idealism, get their priorities wrong from time to time, but they do face facts. Our future lies in their hands. I cannot put this as poetically as the Chinese philosopher who wrote:

'All the flowers and fruits of all tomorrows are in the seeds of today.'

Let us give these seeds good ground in which to grow.

I leave the final words to two of the greatest personalities of this century. They fought the Second World War to its conclusion with all the wit and vigour they possessed; but far from glorifying war, they looked with dread at the possibility of yet another and more terrible conflagration. I quote Field Marshal Montgomery:

'To make a nation great you need religion, you need education, and an educated elite not afraid to take independent lines of thought and action, and who will not merely follow the popular cry. One great fact, the greatest, remains supreme and unassailable. It is this: there are in this world things that are true and things that are false; there are ways that are right and ways that are wrong. There are good men and good women, and there are bad men and bad women. We have to decide which we will follow and make our stand - one or the other we must serve. We can only abolish war by having better men and better women. There is no short cut.'

Last of all I quote the warning words of Winston Churchill, spoken in March 1955:

'It may well be that we shall, by a process of sublime irony, have reached a stage in the story where safety will be the sturdy child of Terror, and Survival the twin brother of Annihilation.'

Let us heed both of these wise men.